THE *Spirituality*
OF NATURE

JIM KALNIN

THE *Spirituality* OF NATURE

Northstone

Concept: Northstone Team
Editor: Ingrid Turnbull
Cover and interior design: Verena Velten and Margaret Kyle
Proofreading: Dianne Greenslade
Photo credits: see page 160

Northstone is an imprint of **Wood Lake Publishing, Inc.** Wood Lake Publishing acknowledges the financial support of the Government of Canada, through the Book Publishing Industry Development Program (BPIDP) for its publishing activities.

At Wood Lake Publishing, we practice what we publish, being guided by a concern for fairness, justice, and equal opportunity in all of our relationships with employees and customers. Wood Lake Publishing is an employee-owned company, committed to caring for the environment and all creation. Wood Lake Publishing recycles, reuses, and encourages readers to do the same. Resources are printed on 100% post-consumer recycled paper and more environmentally friendly groundwood papers (newsprint), whenever possible. A percentage of all profit is donated to charitable organizations.

Library and Archives Canada Cataloguing in Publication

Kalnin, Jim, 1942-
The spirituality of nature / Jim Kalnin.
Includes bibliographical references.
ISBN 978-1-896836-87-4

1. Nature–Religious aspects. 2. Human ecology–Religious aspects. I. Title.
BL65.N35K35 2008   201'.77   C2008-900900-2

Published by Northstone
an imprint of Wood Lake Publishing Inc.
9590 Jim Bailey Road, Kelowna, BC V4V 1R2 Canada
www.woodlakebooks.com
250.766.2778

Printing 10 9 8 7 6 5 4 3 2 1
Printed in Canada

Contents

DEDICATION

To Lois,
who shares my delight with the
infinite wonders of the world,
and makes a brave attempt
to accept some of its
nastier bits.

ACKNOWLEDGMENTS

Writing this book has been a formative learning experience that came to fruition with the generous and patient help of many people. To all of them I owe my gratitude. The varied faces of our planetary home and its numerous, fascinating inhabitants, human and otherwise, also receive my gratitude for what they have taught me.

My wife, Lois Huey-Heck, and my brother Chuck Kalnin were constant guiding lights, each shining in individual ways. Lois' wisdom, clarity, and experience helped me find order in the current of ideas and feelings I waded through to find this book. In all aspects of our life together she continually helps me find my way in and out of the wilderness.

Chuck was in turn encouraging, resourceful, diplomatic, and critical, usually when I needed each of those responses. He gathered many quotes and other resources, contributed his own photographs and writing, read early versions of my manuscript and loaned me a boxful of his most cherished books. His interest and support are greatly appreciated, as are those of the rest of my family.

David Hughes also read the first draft of some chapters and was a real help in bringing life to the stories. His timely responses bumped me out of my habitual pedagogical mode into the realm of the storyteller.

Marilyn Raymond's generosity in sharing her poetry and her enthusiasm for this project are also much appreciated. The world she presents through the existence of frogs expands this body of writing as well as the definitions of spirituality it presents.

The staff at Wood Lake Publishing has been extremely helpful and quite patient as I went through assorted growing pains with this book. Thanks go to Mike Schwartzentruber for his generous help in shaping this volume and in guiding me through the temperamental world of editorial computer software. Margaret Kyle, Verena Velten, and the prepress crew have done their usual magnificent job of complementing the text with a sumptuous visual feast. My deepest gratitude goes to my editor, Ingrid Turnbull, who brought fluidity and clarity to numerous rugged, dense, and foggy patches of writing. She often understood what I was getting at better than I did.

Many others – too many to name – deserve my gratitude for their encouragement, suggestions, and eagerly shared paintings, installations, and photographs.

My lifelong connections to the natural world deepened and intensified during my time in the tiny mountain community of Stocks Meadows. I am eternally grateful to the place and its inhabitants, human and otherwise, who tutored me in the realms of nature, spirituality, and community. Each person, plant, and animal I met there is a cherished member of my extended family, which is now quite large and still expanding.

Introduction

The First Twig

I have this deep and abiding bond with nature that seems to have started when I was quite young.

Some of my earliest memories are of tree branches. I distinctly recall lying in my carriage on warm spring days at my grandfather's homestead beside the Winnipeg River. Grandpa had a small grove of crabapple trees near the riverbank, and I would often be parked in the sunshine beside it. Grandpa's old black dog would curl up beside the carriage and I would doze or watch the dog or stare up into the trees.

In spring, the trees filled with blossoms and fresh new leaves. Sometimes they also filled with my

Auntie. Normally when she came to visit, she would walk along the footpath from her home farther up the river and come through those trees. But sometimes as I lay gazing into a seemingly infinite array of gentle greys, greens, and shimmering whites, parts would suddenly become the brown colour of my auntie's hair, or red like her coat. Then she would step out of the orchard into our yard and bend over my carriage to talk to me. The old black dog would sit up and thump its tail. When her visit was over, my auntie went back into the orchard and merged once again with the trees.

That early memory is a fitting metaphor for our relationship to the natural world. Our ancestors lived in the trees and emerged from them; only unlike my auntie, they didn't visit and then leave. Having come down to the ground, they found that they liked it and decided to stay. Yet they remained connected to the forests.

And so are we. We are all still part of the trees from which we emerged. We are intrinsically tied to them for our air supply and rely on them to provide food, medicine, materials for our homes, and much more, including paper for this book. And our bond with trees goes well beyond the practical, as is evident in many of the stories that follow.

My first years were spent on my parents' small, soil-challenged farm less than an hour's walk from that crabapple orchard. Both their farm and that of my grandfather were close to the town of Lac du Bonnet in southern Manitoba. We lived on the eastern edge of the prairie, right next to the rock country of the Precambrian Shield that covers most of the northeastern section of North America.

When my parents finally gave up their struggle as subsistence farmers, our family moved twenty-seven miles away to Pointe du Boise, a small, hydroelectric company town. There, the Winnipeg River courses through the glaciated and forest-covered hills of the Canadian Shield. Rock bluffs, aspen groves, and the wild turbulent river formed our backyard and were our most influential classrooms, and my brothers and I grew up outdoors as much as possible.

I was fascinated by the contrast between the two distinct geographical regions of prairie and the forested Shield country, and whenever I took the bus between Lac du Bonnet and Pointe du Boise, I would stare out of the bus window, completely captivated, anticipating the landscape change.

*As my eyes search
the prairie I feel
the summer in
the spring.*

Chippewa song

Wheat fields gave way to muskeg and then to spruce forests. As we traveled east, the amount of rock in the few remaining farm fields continually increased until the farms disappeared and there was only rocky expanse. The view filled with low wooded hills, dark, tannin-stained creeks and beaver ponds, and large slabs of granite rock. Lofty mountain ranges had succumbed to several consecutive ice ages and these rocks were all that remained.

Six years later we moved again, this time west across half a conti-nent to Vancouver Island. There, the Pacific Ocean's deep mysteries and the brooding, cedar-cloaked mountain streams filled our summers. These more than made up for the rocky hills we left behind.

We didn't go to church while growing up as my parents were agnostic. They lived lives of generosity and compassion, and maintained a deep respect for the Earth, even when we lived in cities. They planted the early seeds of my own spirituality, seeds that germinated in forests, on mountains, and beside rivers around the world.

When I told my friend David that I was writing a book called *The Spirituality of Nature*, his eyebrows shot up.

"Nature," he mused. "Now there's a tidy little subject!"

Tidy indeed. *Nature* – that would include all animals, plants, humans, microbes, oceans, atmosphere, weather, our planet and solar system, the galaxies, not to mention the intangible parts of the universe, such as dark matter. All academic endeavours – scientific and otherwise, from astronomy to molecular biology to studies of interpersonal behaviour – deal with aspects of nature. Our technologies, industries, and every clever human invention are derived from the natural world. And so are we. Tidy indeed.

Faced with an overwhelming wealth of information concerning different aspects of nature, I found myself relying most on what I had gleaned from personal experience. Even my own limited adventures offer a wide range of definitions of nature.

Many adventures became valuable lessons. When David and I were living in a small community in the Okanagan highlands, we sometimes hiked through the open dry forests to the high ridges above. We would find a rocky cliff edge or the downed trunk of a ponderosa pine tree and sit, gazing out over the panoramic view. To the east was a long section of Okanagan Lake. On clear days we could see

beyond it to several ranges of hills and mountains, the last one a thin, pale blue line of peaks marking where the land met the sky.

David had a monocular that we used to study that expansive view in detail. The monocular also had an attachment that allowed us to see a very different part of the landscape. The first time David attached the extra magnifying lens to the monocular and handed it to me, I used it to look into a crack in the weathered log we sat on.

The tiny crack appeared as a great ravine, with steep sides plummeting down into darkness. Unfamiliar forms of lichen and fungi lined the precipitous walls. I put down the microscope and bent closer to the log. I could barely make out these things with my naked eye. That microscopic view of an ancient tree was my first experience of a changed view of the world.

We took turns discovering minute aspects of nature within the vastness of the hills in which we hiked. More powerful microscopes and telescopes would have revealed even more "worlds," both small and large. Nature expands to embrace infinite possibilities. Ideas about spirituality do the same.

In writing this book, I have drawn from personal experience as if drawing water from a familiar and dependable well. I have then flavoured that water with knowledge gained from the works of great scientists, philosophers, and environmentalists.

When we walk in a forest, we often come home to find that leaves, twigs, burrs, and other bits have hitched a ride with us. In a similar manner, I have collected stories and thoughts from others who likewise learn by wandering out into nature.

1
Pathways into Wilderness

In the small town of Qualicum Beach, on Vancouver Island, spring winds were blowing and cherry blossoms were raining down everywhere. They fell from the ornamental trees that lined the downtown streets, filling the air as they fluttered to the ground. Heaps of bright petals piled up against the curbs, outlining the drab streets with frilly pink borders, and adding a festive feel to the spring day.

The town's inhabitants seemed oblivious to the petals, but as I watched, a boy walking home from school bent down to the curb and scooped up two large handfuls of blossoms. He walked on a bit, looking at them, and then threw

them high in the air and ran full tilt through the fluttering pink cloud as it descended. His peals of laughter filled the street and brought smiles to several faces.

I watched the boy as he continued on into the distance. Every now and then he would pick up more blossoms and repeat the act. He had likely just spent the day sitting at a desk in a relatively quiet classroom with his natural tendencies to run, laugh, and play held in check. When the bell finally rang, he was free, though the day's restraints lingered until he saw those rows of abundant pink petals.

His play was an instinctive thing, a way of balancing the restrictive processes of our education system with the freer animal urges that are still an intrinsic part of our makeup. I found myself hoping that the lad would not lose the impulse to play as he grew older, or that he would somehow manage to get it back if he did. I remembered once seeing someone who seemed to have done just that.

Many years earlier, when I was living in Vancouver, I took a drive around the perimeter of Stanley Park. Although it is a dim echo of what it was before the city grew, the still sizable tract of wilderness offers a needed refuge from the noise and confusion of the city that surrounds it. I drove in pouring rain on a small, dark road between the forest and the ocean. Along the way I passed a playground, deserted except for a man on the swing set. He wore a business suit and was swinging with all his might, his attaché case sitting in a puddle on the pavement beside him. He seemed oblivious to everything as he flew through the air.

I like to think that the boy who ran through the cherry petals will become like that man on the swing when he grows up. I feel that each of them, in their own way, was reaching for something that lies beyond the confines and restrictions of what we call civilization, something that is alive in nature and in us as well. This is human spirituality in very simple terms.

No matter how "civilized" or "cultured" each of us might feel, on a deep level we are still bonded to wilderness. The natural world once held our ancestors in awe and formed the basis of their spiritual beliefs. We may now feel largely disconnected from our evolutionary roots and from those Earth-based spiritual beliefs, but perhaps they remain in our subconscious. I think the boy was impulsively and instinctively looking for more than the fun of throwing cherry petals, and the businessman was seeking something beyond a simple return of childhood innocence.

I get this feeling that most, if not all, of us are seeking the Divine all the time, though perhaps without knowing it. Although some of us consciously seek a reconnection with Spirit, others do so only in a roundabout way. For me, and for many others, fishing is a convoluted, yet rewarding, path to the Divine. We go out onto rivers, ponds, lakes, and oceans thinking the only thing we are after is fish. However, there are times when the beauty and tranquility of those places allow us to see the world and our part in it from a completely different perspective.

When I am out fishing and I bring all of my attention to the present moment, the experience can become very spiritual. Some fishers I know say that connecting to the Divine is the main reason they go. For others, experiencing a heightened spiritual awareness while waving a fishing rod through the air comes as a complete and pleasant surprise.

Most people go fishing all their lives without realizing it's not fish they are after.

Henry David Thoreau

Dawn, who I met while fishing a lake near my home, told me about the epiphany she had when she and her husband, Rick, were fishing on the Adams River. They were fly-casting "egg patterns," fishing for rainbow trout during the Adams River sockeye salmon run. Sockeye salmon spawn annually in this and other rivers along the west side of North America. Trout and other fish from the rivers or adjoining lakes follow them up to the gravel spawning beds and feast on any loose eggs they find. Humans with perhaps too much time on their hands wade in the shallow rivers and cast small hooks covered with pink or orange wool to the trout, hoping to fool them. Real salmon eggs were once used, but their use is now banned in most places.

Dawn and Rick had been fishing downstream from an area of gravel spawning beds. They would slowly wade the shallows, casting their egg imitations upstream and letting them drift to where trout might be holding. A school of large sockeye salmon moved in around Dawn, their behaviour so bound by their biological imperative to reproduce that they were barely aware of her presence in their river. The salmon crowded in all around her, and often bumped into her as they made their way upstream.

Dawn found this quite unsettling and fought the urge to return to shore. She told herself that these large, red, hook-jawed creatures were not a danger to her, or even remotely interested in her. She grew accustomed to their presence and before long started to enjoy their company. When she no lon-

ger felt afraid, something shifted in her. She became overwhelmed with a sense of awe and wonder unlike anything she had felt before. She realized she was surrounded by a miracle of life and death. She could only describe her reaction as a kind of holy reverence.

She stood there in the river for some time, no longer fishing. Eventually her ecstatic state of awareness faded and she began to fish again. Her husband told me later that Dawn caught and released a five-pound rainbow trout that afternoon. It was her biggest trout ever, but the excitement and significance of that catch were minor in comparison to her privileged encounter with the salmon migration.

There is something truly miraculous about phenomena in nature like the annual epic spawning migrations of salmon and other fish. Sockeye salmon spawn in rivers like the Adams each fall, with the eggs hatching the following spring. The fry then move to nearby "nursery" lakes for their first year of life. As yearlings, they follow the current down to the Pacific Ocean. Those that survive that journey spend most of their lives in the ocean, leaving only to return to their birth streams to spawn and die. The other Pacific salmon (coho, pinks, chums, and in some rivers, chinooks) also migrate to salt water during their first year of life. There they grow to huge sizes because of the abundant supplies of food, such as plankton and herring, available to them.

The journey from the open ocean to the river spawning ground can take several weeks and is fraught with hardship and peril. Once the salmon enter fresh water, they generally stop eating and live off stored fat. Their natural instinct of self-preservation is replaced with a single-minded determination to reach their spawning grounds at all costs.

Their bodies go through spectacular transformations. The males of all salmon species develop hooked jaws; some get pronounced humps on their backs, and some change colours. The bodies of sockeye salmon turn bright red, while their heads remain a dark, earthy green. The sight of brilliant red fish against the rich gold and brown colours of the riverbed is spectacular.

The drama and beauty of these fish, and the clear mountain rivers they swim in, ignite our souls. Their determination to complete their journey against all odds can also inspire us in relation to overcoming our own obstacles and reaching our goals. So compelling are these annual spawning displays that many people travel to the rivers each fall to witness this miracle of life and death. Predators such as bears, eagles, mink, and ravens come as well, for the nourishment of their bodies if not their souls.

Nature can get under our skin. And it often surprises us with a different vision of the world than what we are expecting. Dawn's transformative experience on the Adams River reminds us that some of the unexpected turns that our lives take in fact bring us to what we have been seeking. While we may approach wilderness with our own expectations and agendas, wilderness might have other ideas. Rivers provide us with so much more than fishing, and forests and mountains offer us an abundance that goes far beyond the joy of skiing or hiking.

I grew up with my brothers, Chuck, Phil, and Lanny, mainly in rural locations. Rivers, mud, and frozen ponds probably taught us as much as our years of schooling, and in some ways more.

Once, while we were all swimming in the Winnipeg River, we caught a turtle that was missing one hind leg. We imagined the narrow escape that the turtle must have had, eluding a northern pike or other predator. The turtle had lost a leg but it had survived, thanks to quick reflexes and a smooth, hard shell. Encounters in the natural world like that one did much to develop in us a sense of awe at the miracle and resilience of life. I think my reverence for all life started there.

We spent countless glorious summer days up in trees or building huts in the bush, and cold winter evenings skating, tobogganing, and tunneling into snow banks. We became "experts" on the structural properties of snow during the different phases of winter, and learned much about the local species of grasshoppers, worms, and frogs. The bits of nature we dragged home daily further enhanced our relationship to the land, while causing extra work and a few surprises for our mother. Washing our clothes became a series of biological studies for her as well as she discovered the things we had left in the pockets of our blue jeans.

Our childhood environment shapes our adult life, whether we grow up on a small prairie farm or in a Manhattan apartment. The values our parents instilled in us, such as honesty and a respect for all life, complemented what we learned from the great outdoors. Our parents provided for us well, although they had neither the money nor the inclination to buy us all the latest toys. Learning to "make do" was part of our family credo. When we wrecked our electric train set, there was no replacement. So we spent lots of time entertaining ourselves in nature and thus deepening that bond. An interest in nature, and an ease and familiarity with the outdoors, have followed all four of us into adulthood.

My brother Phil's real passion is airplanes. He owns and flies a vintage World War II Harvard trainer, and his wife, Lee, flies her own plane, a small Cessna. Flying is a great passion, but so is the land below them. While they are soaring high above the ground in a world made of light, they also appreciate the beauty of the world below viewed from new perspectives. And flying gives them quick access to remote places of real beauty. Their typical holiday consists of flying to a distant airport or isolated beach, where they moor their plane and pitch their tent. They carry light-weight camping gear and under-sized, collapsible mountain bikes that they use to go exploring. And while flying frees them from the Earth and gives them the soaring eagle's view of the world, they also cherish the small and intimate details. When we went to visit them at their home recently, they were as excited as children to show us the small green frog which had taken up residence in the spout of their bamboo water fountain.

The uniqueness of aerial views of our world has inspired many besides Phil and Lee. Canadian artist Toni Onley flew his own aircraft for many years, and the altered perspective affected and inspired his artwork in many ways. He made large abstracted collages and small serigraph prints that were inspired by the shapes of lakes, rocks, trees, and mountains as seen from above. The minimalist form that he developed in those early works became the guiding force behind his better known essential and spiritual watercolour landscape paintings.

Scattered Landscape, 2003
Toni Onley
Mixed Media
22" x 30"

The ocean depths or the heights of space flight offer us dramatically different viewpoints to those of everyday life on Earth. Many astronauts find that their lives have been completely changed by the experience of their space flight. The sight of Earth as a small blue and white ball floating in a black void has a profound affect on many, and may be an emblem for our changing global consciousness. For years I kept a large image of the Earth rising over the horizon of the moon on my office wall. It worked wonders as a reality check against bureaucratic entanglements and campus politics.

If the landscape reveals one certainty, it is that the extravagant gesture is the very stuff of creation.

Annie Dillard

Of all my brothers, Lanny's career is most closely connected to his childhood interests. He started fishing when he was about three years old, and has never stopped. He has worked for the Department of Fisheries and Oceans for almost all his adult life, and has spent as much time on rivers and the Pacific Ocean as in an office.

Early in his career he conducted research on spawning salmon using a method called "dead pitch." Lanny would wade into the spawning creeks with a *peugh*, a pitchfork with only one tine, and a hand-held

counter. When he counted a salmon that had died after it spawned, he would use the *peugh* to pitch it onto the bank so it wouldn't get counted twice. Grizzly bears and other creatures followed him and snacked on the fish he threw onto the bank. Although a grizzly treed him once, they mostly ignored him, or at least tolerated his presence. Lanny says he got somewhat used to them, though he couldn't stop sneaking peeks over his shoulder as he worked. Despite the bears, he loved the work. Most of his holidays are still spent fishing or camping with his wife, Cathy.

Standing in a river for the better part of a day is something I have done as well, though not with bears hanging about expecting lunch. Whenever the fish aren't biting, I watch the land around me. Staying in one place for some time brings that place into sharper focus and enhances my sense of spiritual connection. The more I look at the rocks, trees, birds, and animals, the more I discover about their nature. I might eventually notice elusive creatures like rock pikas, or perceive how the trees grow much more densely in a damp location than in a drier one upriver. I might realize that the squirrel running across the rocks has one ear missing, likely from a close encounter with a hawk. Seeing the details makes the forests, rivers, and lakes feel like home.

Revisiting a spot also deepens and expands our awareness of it. Photographer Freeman Patterson suggests to students that they return regularly to a favourite location. This allows them to see that part of the world through its many changes and to better appreciate its totality. Drawing or painting from nature requires focused attention for substantial periods of time, which helps deepen our connection while nourishing our souls. I encourage even those with little drawing practice to draw the places they like. Drawing as prayer or meditation works to deepen our bonds, once we let go of the goal of making "good art" and allow ourselves simply to absorb everything we see as we draw it.

My eldest brother, Chuck, worked at agriculture research stations until he retired. Now he chases butterflies and creeps up on flowers with a camera. Nature photography is one of his passions, and butterflies hold a special place within that interest.

When I e-mailed him to ask him what was spiritual about this, he wrote: "The butterfly starts out as an egg laid on the underside of leaves by the female. It grows into a caterpillar that can be seen inching itself slowly along a plant stem. It then enters its chrysalis or pupa stage. None of these stages is especially attractive, visually. But then something miraculous happens. The butterfly emerges, fluttering along the hillside, exposing the exquisite beauty that was hidden till then."

The spiritual symbolism Chuck sees in butterflies is shared by many of us. The transformation from caterpillar to butterfly has long been an inspiration. We might hope for a parallel of spiritual transformation for ourselves.

Butterflies have a more personal significance to Chuck as well. He lost his wife, Elaine, to cancer recently, and butterflies had long held a special attraction for her. They are now a reminder of her joy and a bridge back to their time together. He says that he always feels closer to Elaine when butterflies are around.

There are numerous devices through which we can temporarily escape the complexities of life. Anything from flower petals and swing sets to fishing tackle or airplanes can help us break the bonds of civilization and soar in the sunlit clouds for a while. They may even take us beyond the limits of our own expectations.

All of life is invested with spirit and with intelligence. Watching things grow, compete, propagate, and then die a natural death helps us to see the bigger picture. We may then realize that there is much more to us than deadlines, agendas, goals, and possessions. Each of us exists as an individual, and as a strand in the web of life. Becoming more aware of how we are connected to nature not only nourishes us; it strengthens and honours the Earth as well.

2

Wilderness as Sanctuary

FINDING A CATHEDRAL

Living in a large city after growing up in the country can definitely alter one's frame of mind. After I graduated from the Vancouver School of Art, I stayed in the city for some time. I had a decent job and got along fairly well with my employers and co-workers. Vancouver itself had lots of charm; it is a modest city nestled in a spectacular natural setting between lofty blue mountains and a gentle sea. The large and historic Fraser River meets the ocean here.

But I wasn't very happy. I found my job boring and the city depress-ing and I lacked the impetus to change either my job or where I lived. I would have preferred to live someplace greener and quieter, but that would have meant moving and looking for work. So I stayed where I was and whined about it to any-one who would listen.

My friend Hugh was a good lis-tener. He was listening to me one autumn afternoon as we walked through the wet streets under dark clouds. Sirens wailed; someone we couldn't see shouted in the back-ground, and I could hear glass breaking behind us. I was com-

plaining about the constant noise when Hugh suddenly shot ahead of me. He scooped up a crumpled candy wrapper that was lying on the sidewalk, and caught up to the man walking in front of us. He tapped him on the shoulder.

"Excuse me," he said in a polite voice. "But you dropped this."

The guy glared at him. Hugh smiled. The guy looked at the candy wrapper in Hugh's outstretched hand. Hugh kept smiling and holding it out to him. Eventually the other man took the wrapper, stuffed it in his pocket, and walked away.

I caught up to Hugh, grinning now.

"That was hilarious!" I said. "The look on his face was priceless. I actually thought he might hit you, but he just took the wrapper!"

"Well, he dropped it," Hugh deadpanned, "and I thought he might like to have it back."

"This city needs more guys like you, Hugh. Then it might be a decent place to live. Look at all the crap on the street!"

We walked on, our mood buoyant despite the steadily increasing volume of rain. Hugh had grown up in the city and it never got to him as it did me.

We found a decent coffee shop and went in. The talk soon turned to fishing. Hugh had just bought a very nice bamboo fly rod.

"We should go camping on the Skagit River," he stated. "Good-sized trout there."

"Yeah, sounds good," I said. "But let's go for more than a weekend. Otherwise we spend more time hauling stuff around than enjoying ourselves. Hey, I get Monday off in a couple weeks and work is slow, so I could always miss Tuesday and say I was sick."

We were warming to this idea when Hugh's face suddenly clouded.

"Aahh! Can't do it," he said. "Nan and I have interviews with the adoption agency then. Look, why don't you go anyway? You'll do fine by yourself, you know your way around the woods. And if the fishing's good, we can try to get there together later on."

I thought about this for a while and it started to feel like a pretty good idea. Hugh began giving me directions to the place, describing the small gravel road that would lead me there. He cautioned me to watch for it shortly after entering Manning Park.

I stopped him.

"You forget, Hugh, that I don't have a car."

"Yeah, right. So take the bus!"

Hugh saw solutions as easily as I saw problems.

"It's only three hours from here. Ask the bus driver to let you off at the little logging road at the beginning of the big bend going into Rhododendron Flats. Also ask him to look for you on the return trip on the day you want to come back. Find out what time the bus will be passing and make sure you are there waiting for it. Easy!"

A few days later I stood clinging to a stanchion in the aisle of a city bus jammed with people as wet as I was. The bus careened in and out of the traffic and I was kept upright more by the press of bodies than from my grip on the metal pole. Wendy, a co-worker, was on the same bus, and when she spotted me she wedged her way toward me though the press of commuters. We talked about the rain and work, and then I told her I was going camping in the Skagit Valley.

"Alone?" she asked.

"Yeah, sure," I answered.

"So where is this place?"

I described its location and told her a bit about the country. She thought about that for a moment.

"I couldn't do that," she said. "Just the idea that there are wild animals, like bears and cougars, that would stop me dead cold. I

couldn't relax with that. Hey, and what if you hurt yourself?"

Eight days later I was hanging onto a stanchion and swaying under my pack, this time at the front of a Greyhound bus as it wound its way along the wet highway. The bus slowed down as it approached the gravel road just before the big turn into Rhododendron Flats.

"Here?" the driver asked.

I nodded. The bus pulled off the pavement onto the gravel shoulder and stopped by the overgrown dirt road that ran off into the trees. It was pouring rain and getting dark.

"You sure?" he asked again.

I hesitated, then said, "Yeah, sure."

I stepped down to the road-side and the bus door hissed shut behind me. I stood in the rain and watched the bus swing back out onto the asphalt, thinking that maybe I should still be on it. Then I shouldered my pack and walked into the forest.

I followed the dirt road until the highway sounds faded. I could hear the river on my right and turned towards it. I stumbled through bracken and over wet rocks until I found a flat spot on which to pitch my tent. It was dark when I had finished, and I was wet, hungry, and feeling a little overwhelmed.

I stood straight and took a deep breath. The air was full of fresh and clean forest smells: mushrooms, earth, and flowers. Rain pooled on unseen tree branches above me and then fell to the ground with resounding smacks. But beyond the rain sounds the forest was quiet. Almost too quiet; I realized that I missed the constant city noises I had come here to escape. I tilted my face up to the rain and stood there by my tent for quite some time, absorbing the quiet solitude along with the raindrops.

A loud sound, like a branch snapping, immediately dissolved the peace of the forest. Images of bears and cougars insinuated themselves into my thoughts as I searched the darkness around me. I remembered hearing about a family who had held a reunion at a nearby cabin. They had built a large bonfire under the big fir tree in the yard and roasted hotdogs and marshmallows and took lots of flash photos. Weeks later, when

the pictures were developed, they saw a full-grown cougar stretched out on a large branch of the fir tree about ten feet above their heads. It had apparently been there right through the evening, and they had never noticed.

I listened for more forest sounds, but the next thing I heard was my own muttering about what a dumb idea it was to come here. I then went inside the tent, dried my hair with a towel, ate sardines out of a tin with my fingers, crawled into my sleeping bag, and fell asleep.

I awoke quite refreshed and saw that it was still raining. I climbed out of the tent and stretched. Large ferns, mushrooms, and wild ginger neatly bordered my tent, as if landscaped. Behind them stood a group of large cedar trees. Very large cedar trees. Each one took up more space on the ground than my tent did. Their tops were lost in the rich green canopy overhead. The falling rain hazed that canopy to a soft green glow. Light seemed to radiate from everything.

It rained for my whole stay there. The steep mountains, cloud cover, and dense forest kept the valley quite dark, but as I made my way through it my mood slowly got lighter. I found myself looking up moss and lichen covered tree trunks and smiling. Each tiny strand and flake of the things that grew on those trunks glowed in the muted light. The cumulative effect was that the whole forest radiated green, gold, and silver. This place spoke to me of slow grace and ancient wisdom; things that I would spend most of my life trying to understand.

I caught no fish and after a while quit trying. I ate cold food out of packages and cans, due to difficulties keeping a fire going. I occasionally heard sounds in the forest and imagined large animals, though I saw only squirrels and two deer. One evening I looked up from throwing some dry split cedar on a rare successful fire and saw the deer standing not far away in the glow. They hadn't made a sound. We watched each other for some time; then they turned and became shadows. I stared after them and sighed. There was a deep peace in that valley and it was entering my soul.

When the wind blows, that is my medicine,
When it rains, that is my medicine,
When it hails, that is my medicine,
When it becomes clear after a storm, that is my medicine.

– Anonymous

On the third day, when I walked to the road to wait for the bus, it was still raining and I was still wet. I turned and waved goodbye to the forest as I climbed up the bank to the highway. The open roadway was much brighter than the forest; I felt as if I had just emerged from a dark building. A church perhaps? But on looking back at the graceful rise of the cedar trees and the flowing curves of their branches, I amended that thought; no mere church, this place, but a cathedral.

I soon started to go to the Skagit Valley on a regular basis; so often, in fact, that it began to feel like home. I went there with various friends, though somehow never with Hugh, and often I went alone. Each visit made my life in the city more bearable, as I learned to bring my relaxation back from the valley with me.

The fishing turned out to be quite good in the Skagit, as Hugh had promised. So were the edible wild mushrooms, berries, and wild ginger. These things were not what pulled me back there though. These trips became my spiritual pilgrimage, putting my feet on a path that I am still following.

I hardly ever camp there now; closer wilderness sanctuaries fill that need. Cathedrals full of green and silver light come in many shapes and locations. But whenever my wife, Lois, and I drive to Vancouver along the Hope-Princeton Highway, we try to stop there for a while. We follow a new road in that takes us directly to a parking lot built right on the spot where I made my first camp. There we take a breather by the river. If we're not racing to catch a ferry to Vancouver Island, we walk down the trail for a few kilometers, me waving my arms and telling Lois stories until the presence of that place silences me, and I remember it is enough just to be there.

Oh silvery morn, without a fail,
your dawn unfolds a timeless tale;
of haunted ships with hazy sails,
with ghostly rows and masts so pale.

Eerie shadows,
misty and frail,
tossed upon a swirling gale.

The fog-ships came from where all
dreams hail,
to appear every morn without avail;
leaving behind but a dew-laden trail.

-RUTH BALDINGER

A Square Foot of Sanity

Sanctuary need not be a set of buildings or a river valley. One troubled pilgrim I knew found inner peace inside a square foot of ground. Claude was a recluse; he lived mainly in opposition to the rest of society. He often lived alone in the forest, because spending any length of time with other people inevitably led to trouble.

Sometimes he would drive his old school bus off-road to a remote place where others were unlikely to follow, and spend winter snowbound high in the mountains. He saw no one for months, lived on dried and canned food, and cut firewood by hand for his small airtight stove.

Other times, he lived in less isolated situations. He spent a year or so in the small community in the hills where I lived. His rough edges quickly became apparent and relationships with him became guarded. I was his closest neighbour

and saw him frequently, which gave me several opportunities to witness a very different side of him.

He started to tell me about his nature studies. Claude related how he would do these on a regular basis, using a technique common to biology students and researchers. He would walk out into a forest and stop. Then he would bend down and push four small wooden stakes into the ground, describing a one foot square. He then tied fine thread from stake to stake, marking out his area of study. Over several days, he would study these small plots on the forest floor in minute detail, and make careful notes on what he found.

When he talked to me about his discoveries in these plots, the hard lines on his face softened and his eyes lit up. He would describe how he carefully lifted each leaf to find the insects, small mushrooms, or animal droppings that were nestled underneath. In one plot, he might find a dozen different kinds of

insect and several species of moss. He occasionally found tiny white bones and claimed he could distinguish miniature, insect-sized "game trails" worn into the ground cover.

"There are many stories hidden there on the ground," he said. "Who knows what happened there? All kinds of secrets are waiting for us to discover them, all over the forest. If you take the time and observe carefully, they will teach you what you need to know about life."

Claude's square foot studies did something else besides teach him about life. They were keys to the door that unlocked his long buried innocence and sense of wonder. Perhaps those intense nature studies were his only way back there. The critical stances he had developed as an adult gave way when he ventured into these small and intimate places.

Like Claude, many others have benefited from time alone in the wilderness. Immersing myself in forests certainly gave me confidence that I sorely lacked as a youth. Facing my fears and becoming self-reliant has made running the gamut of the rules of etiquette easier. At times, though, I think I might choose a confrontation with a bear over some of the sticky social situations that occur. At least bears, though not always predictable, are pretty straightforward creatures.

People have been going off into the woods alone on spiritual quests for eons, and usually faced more danger and hardships than I have done. Spiritual or vision quests often involved elements of fasting and freezing. There were no wilderness guides or Gortex jackets when Jesus went into the wilderness, or when a pubescent Algonquin boy was left alone on a mountain for a week. While hiking in good boots with a pack full of freeze-dried gourmet meals and a sub-zero sleeping bag may be the way to go, it is less likely to bring visions or insights that permanently alter our reality.

Yet all the experiences we have in nature are of value to us. They can help us heal physically, emotionally, and intellectually, and our ties to the Creator may be strengthened simply through close encounters with Creation itself.

3

The Pond and the Universe

The small, high altitude lake where I canoed one sunny September day had a few other fly fishers out on it as well. Beyond them, I noticed an elderly couple in a small rowboat heading in my direction. The man was rowing fast with all his might, while the woman sat hunched forward on the rear seat with both of her arms up, holding an open newspaper over her head. I could see the tension in them from across the lake.

Although there were no clouds in the sky, there were raindrop-sized splashes in the water around the rowboat. The splashes occurred only over that section of the lake and seemed to be moving along

with the boat. It reminded me of how localized rainstorms advance across the surface of water.

But this was no weather phenomenon. These were the water

boatmen – small bugs that don't fly much, but make it a notable event when they do. Similar events occur annually on lakes, ponds, and slow moving creeks all over the world.

Water boatmen live most of their one-year life cycle in the water. They start there as eggs laid on submerged stems and leaves. The eggs hatch and become nymphs that then grow through five separate stages, or "instars." By the last stage, the insects have fully developed wings and are capable of flight. That is when they leave the pond or lake and fly into the woods to mate. Within a short time, the females return to re-enter the water in their spectacular kamikaze fashion, diving to the depths to lay eggs.

These insects can be quite prolific, and with thousands of them simultaneously hurtling full speed at the water, they adequately imitate a good size rain shower. This is quite a sight to behold and not actually a suicide attempt on their part.

Rather, the boatmen do this in order to break through the surface tension of the water. Since the surface film is strong enough to allow some insects to walk on it or hang suspended under it, it can present a formidable barrier. Some boatmen are able to break through it with a big splash, while others fail to penetrate it and can be seen spinning across the water's surface. They then scrabble around in an attempt to get through, although such efforts often attract the trout and the tiny insects disappear in a swirling boil of water.

The couple in the rowboat hadn't been fishing, and seemed both puzzled and disturbed by the "bug fall" they were witnessing. On the other hand, the fly fishers knew exactly what was happening and reacted accordingly. Rowboats, canoes, and small inflatable water craft were propelled rapidly toward that part of the lake where the splashes were occurring. The fishers knew that the trout would already be there, feasting on the boatmen.

I could see one fly fisher changing the fly pattern on his line, and felt sure that he was tying on an imitation of a boatman.

A sunny fall day, usually after the first frost, is a likely time to witness these "nuptial flights," though with patient observation the nymphs can be seen in the water throughout the spring and summer. Like the winged adults, the mature nymphs are mainly air breathers. They forage underwater and return regularly to the surface to replenish their air supply, trapping it between the fine hairs along their abdomens. The tiny boatmen, barely more than a quarter inch long, rise to the surface and dive again in a fraction of a second, holding their replenished bubble of air. These insect scuba divers easily propel themselves through the water with their hind legs, which, being also fringed with fine hairs, are quite efficient "oars."

I first learned about water boatmen (and many other insects)

through my interest in fly fishing, and now find the insects themselves at least as engaging as the art of pursuing trout. There is a comical quality to the underwater antics of water boatmen, not to mention their aerial maneuvers, which I find especially appealing. Like the migrating salmon, their biological drive to reproduce is so powerful that they pay little attention to self-preservation. They will fly unheedingly into anything that looks wet, including swimming pools, ditches, rain puddles, and newly poured cement.

When we see this wild abandon and zest for life in such creatures, it can spark a sense of deep connection to the larger world. Wild creatures have an unconscious ease in their relationship to their world that we humans seem to have lost; watching a creature in its element can let us awaken to our own deep-rooted sense of oneness.

Quiet contemplations of Earth's creatures can also slow us down and heal us. Jesus spent time simply watching birds fly and flowers grow. When he said, "Consider the lilies of the field, how they grow; they toil not, neither do they spin" (Mathew 6:28), he was reminding us of something important. We can live fulfilled, rewarding lives without a lot of deadlines and commitments. Walt Whitman echoed Jesus' teaching in many of his poems with his reminders of the importance of being "idle." Whitman himself spent many pleasant afternoons sitting by creeks and gazing upon meadows in contemplation.

As a race, we don't seem to know this. Or perhaps we have forgotten what we once understood. In our daily haste, we miss things of value. We strive so hard to build our wealth and future security that we become addicted to the striving and find it hard to stop. We lose sight of the truth – which is that the fulfillment we seek is not in a distant future, but right here, in the present moment, all around us.

Creatures in the wild do indeed toil and spin, although it doesn't come off as such. They work and strive in order to survive, but they do it intuitively and in sync with their surroundings. No ulterior motives, hidden agendas, guidebooks, instructions, rules of eti-

quette, or bylaws. There is much we can learn, or relearn, from nature, even from tiny creatures imitating raindrops. I like to think that if Jesus ever saw the water boatmen crashing headlong into the water during their nuptial flights, he would have enjoyed "considering" them as much as I do.

I want to go soon and live away by the pond, where I shall only hear the wind whispering among the reeds. It will be successful if I shall have left myself behind.

– Henry David Thoreau

And with water we have made all living things

Water that collects in a depression in the ground will become filled with life in short order. Algae, fungi, and bacteria quickly establish themselves and become important building blocks in the pond's life. Marginal plants that don't mind wet feet will creep to the water's edge, where they will grow and die seasonally and add nutrients to the water and soil. Other plants will head past them right into that nutrient-enriched water. Everything that lives and dies there contributes something to the microcosmic world of the pond.

Worms, insects, amphibians, and fish complicate the mix when they arrive. They in turn attract birds, reptiles, and mammals, further upsetting the balance and inadvertently contributing to a new one. Each new plant or animal that finds the environment to its liking will change the overall dynamic of the pond when it moves in.

Everything that thrives there does so at a cost to something else. Conversely, everything contributes to the support of other lives. Thus food chains are formed. Because most creatures in a pond consume more than one other kind of life, and are in turn a food source for several other creatures, food chains become linked and create complex interdependencies. I sometimes try to follow the links in a food chain when I have the time to hang around a pond. It seems a marvel that one chain might start with algae or diatoms and in only a few short steps end up as a heron or a moose.

My lifelong fascination with the inner workings of streams, lakes, and ponds has followed me home to influence the shape and content of our yard. Lois and I have built fairly extensive water features.

One is a small pond from which water is pumped uphill to the top of a thirty-foot "creek." The water splashes over a series of waterfalls, slides gracefully around the roots of fir trees and past flowerbeds, and then tumbles back down to the rock-lined pond. We also built a reflecting pond next to it. The two ponds are not connected and have become distinctly different environments.

The waterfall pond grows several related kinds of algae but attracts very few insects. The algae growth is quite prolific; I remove masses of it regularly so that it doesn't fill the pond and clog the pump. The still pond, a few feet away, grows only one (slightly different) species of algae. In early spring, bright green clouds of it grow profusely on all parts of the pond. As the weather warms, and the numerous and varied insect populations grow, this forest of green filaments gets consumed, and by summer there is only a faint hint of green adhering to the small rocks.

This spring, however, I noticed a few small water bug larvae in the reflecting pond. They are our first carnivorous pond creatures, and they have noticeably changed the dynamics in the microenvironment. They eat enough of the other herbivorous larvae and pupae to allow the algae forest to thrive through the summer, but in a controlled manner. Nature tends towards establishing a balance wherever possible.

As other plants and insects move in, the interrelationships will shift again. I find myself eagerly anticipating the growth of a more complex pond community that incorporates several food chains, although our ponds will likely never be able to feed a heron or a moose.

Meanwhile, any new addition catches our attention and interest. Lois and I spotted a red dragonfly resting on a rock beside the reflecting pond and are hoping it was there to lay eggs.

We are all familiar with the miraculous transformation that occurs when a caterpillar becomes a butterfly. We may find parallels to this event in our own lives, both literally and figuratively. Recalling the beauty of butterflies and the miracle of change have helped many to face the pain of their own difficult transitions. Butterflies helped my brother Chuck through the pain of his loss and led him out into the fields more often.

Insects such as dragonflies and damselflies are all the more captivating because they are not shrouded in cocoons during their transformation to winged adult. When a dragonfly nymph is ready to metamorphose, usually at night, it will slowly climb out of the water onto a tree or plant stem. It then performs the amazing feat of splitting open along its back and crawling out of itself. It does this by tightly gripping a tree branch and pumping blood to the thorax. The thorax swells and causes the outer skin of the dragonfly nymph to split open. Through a series of convolutions, and with the help of its new legs, the adult dragonfly slowly emerges. It can take up to twelve hours before it is ready to fly away.

Damselflies usually emerge in much shorter order and in the early morning. The nymph climbs onto a lily pad or reed near shore and performs its amazing feat there. Damselflies are often a pale yellow-brown colour when they first emerge, but before long their skins harden and their abdomens turn the familiar blue.

The opportunity to observe this miracle of damselfly transformation is enough to get me out of bed and to the lake earlier than usual, while watching dragonflies emerge requires me to work the night shift. I have yet to scour the darkened shoreline with a flashlight in order to watch the transformation in dragonflies, but I have been lucky enough to see one emerging when I happened to still be out on a lake just after dark. I likely will never tire of watching these amazing creatures slowly straighten out, unfold and expand their new wings, and fly away.

The life cycles of insects are tiny echoes of what is taking place on an intergalactic scale. The much larger "ponds" that we call galaxies have their own cyclical changes, as does each celestial body within them.

The phenomena we know as supernovae are the result of stars exploding. The clouds of debris resulting from the star deaths become the birthplaces of new stars and planets. These clouds are called nebulae, and they contain all the basic elements for life as we know it.

The scientific story of Creation tells us that everything started as a singularity – something incredibly hot and dense and believed to be about the size of a pinhead. This singularity had all the matter that now exists concentrated inside it. It is believed to have flared forth into the void as hot dense plasma over 15 billion years ago.

As the plasma cooled, hydrogen and helium formed and eventually concentrated into densely packed clouds. Scientists believe this happened in response to the gravitational forces exerted by dark matter. The concentration of particles in each cloud grew so dense that it ignited into a star. The first galaxies were usually single stars surrounded by clouds of gas.

With each succeeding generation, the substance of the universe grew more complex. Just as expired pond creatures add nourishment to their environment for future generations and for a greater diversity, so do the inhabitants of galaxies, though of course at a very different pace and on a vastly different scale. The "nutrients" from for-

We are nothing but flowers in a flowering universe
– Nakagawa Soen Roshi

mer stars become the life source for succeeding generations. They also allow other forms of celestial beings to evolve and exist. All the planets in our solar system formed out of a nebula that resulted from the death of a nearby star. And the cosmic metamorphosis is still ongoing.

The well-studied crab nebula is the remnant of a supernova so bright it was visible in daylight. The event was recorded by both Chinese and Arab astronomers in 1054 CE. The supernova was apparently visible for about two years, but when it died down the resulting nebula could no longer be seen. No one knew it was still there until John Bevis observed it in 1731. Today, with the help of sophisticated research tools such as the Hubble Space Telescope, astronomers are discovering much about it. And from it they are gaining great insights into the very fabric of the universe.

Astronomers now have telescopes so powerful that they can view galaxies billions of light years away.

That means they are actually looking into the past and seeing some of those primordial galaxies as they existed near the beginning of time.

While looking out into space can give us information and new perspectives on our own lives, we can learn as much by carefully observing the minutiae of life here on this small planet. What we see when we watch a dragonfly nymph transform into a winged adult is an extension of the dynamic that includes the birthing of planets, stars, and galaxies. As the universe moves, so does each tiny part. We see change taking place both up close and far away. We watch the universe unfolding.

When we look up at the stars, we are in a real sense watching a part of ourselves. When we watch raindrops or water boatmen splash onto the surface of a pond, what we see is an integral part of our own lives. Inasmuch as we are individuals, we are also part of the greater whole. In fact, our very existence relies on this interdependency.

Although human beings habitually view themselves as separate entities, isolated inside their own skins and thoughts, the separation is an illusion. We cause trouble for ourselves when we believe we are alone, unappreciated, misunderstood, or different from others. It happens because we forget all our connections. We lose our awareness of being part of the big picture. I can think of no better cure for these states of *dis-ease* than to spend a night sitting on a mountain or by a lake, staring up at the sky, watching the galaxy move.

New Perspective on an Old Story

Humans throughout history have pondered existence. Most cultures have evolved stories to explain the mystery of how we got here and why we are here. Most of these stories hold to the belief that the universe and all life were created by some sort of Higher Power.

Humanity's creation stories are now experiencing an extreme makeover at the hand of contemporary science. But some of the credibility given the latest scientific version of Creation may result from the fact that we find in it a number of parallels to the creation stories of old. Because of its familiarity, it feels "real," or true.

In the beginning God created Heaven and the Earth.

Many creation stories start out with nothing. There exists a great void that the Creator then fills. One ancient Chinese creation story

Originating power brought forth a universe.

– Thomas Berry

starts with all Creation trapped inside a cosmic egg. When the shell is breached, everything is released.

The book of Genesis declares that God "spoke" the world into existence. This is a common occurrence in creation stories. Some African traditions vary this idea by having the Supreme Being vomit us forth. Either way, we end up issuing from the mouth of the Creator.

The Babylonian *Enuma Elish,
the Epic of Creation*, found written
on seven tablets at Nineveh (now
Musul, Iraq), has much in common to the story told in the Judeo-
Christian scriptures.

When on high the heaven was
    not named,
And the earth beneath did not
    yet bear a name,
And the primeval Apsu,
    who begat them,
And chaos Tiamat, the mother
    of them both,
Their waters were mingled
    together,

And no field was formed,
    no marsh was to be seen,
When of the gods none had
    been called into being
And none bore a name, and no
    destinies were ordained;
Then were created the gods in
    the midst of heaven.[1]

The *Tao Te Ching*, written by Lao
Tsu in the sixth century BCE,
echoes the *Enuma Elish* when it
speaks of a void beyond all existence, and once again explains Creation as being "told."

The Tao that can be told is not
    the eternal Tao
The name that can be named is
    not the eternal name
The nameless is the beginning
    of heaven and earth
The named is the mother of ten
    thousand things

Before the big bang, or flaring forth,
(or telling, or vomiting) of matter from the singularity, there was
nothing. Time and space did not
exist. The Heavens had not been

---

[1] *Enuma Elish*, www.sacred-texts,com/ane/enuma.htm

named. This is what many creation stories have told us, and present day astronomy seems to concur. Scientists are coming to believe that the singular event that brought the physical universe into being simultaneously created space and time.

Most of the ancient stories tell of the creation of life as well as the creation of the universe and many parallel the scientific story of how life began. Ancient or modern, the stories tell us that, physically speaking, we all come from the Earth and are sustained by it.

In one Haida myth, the trickster Raven finds the humans in a clamshell. A Choctaw legend tells us the Creator made humans from the "primal mound," after which they crawled up a long tunnel to daylight. In the Biblical account, God fashioned the first human "of dust from the soil" and then breathed life into his nostrils. Scientists say life started in the world's oceans, in what is referred to as "primal soup."

Before life began, the seas became filled with water that formed in the atmosphere and rained down onto Earth. Water collected first on the land and then flowed down to the seas, carrying minerals with it.

Other elements that were needed to start life on Earth came directly from space in the form of interstellar dust. Repeated heating and cooling of these dust particles resulted in the formation of many and varied molecules on their surfaces. The enhanced dust would adhere to comets, some of which eventually plummeted to

Earth. The supercharged stardust thus became a primal soup ingredient and is part of our global ancestry.

Other important particles were likely created when water from the oceans seeped into deep thermal vents in the Earth's crust and became intensely heated. The transformed particles then made their way back to the oceanic stockpot as additional seasoning.

These altered elements from vastly different sources eventually merged into molecules. When the primordial seas accumulated the right mix of necessary ingredients – such as acids, sugars, and nucleotides – biomolecules, with the unique ability to replicate, are said to have formed. From these sprang the first primitive cells, called prokaryotes.

From the prokaryotes, more advanced, complex forms of cells developed. One line of cells that evolved were the eukaryotes, from which came most life forms, including microorganisms, fungi, plants, animals, and humans. That makes the eukaryotes our first true ancestors. And since everything alive – each dandelion, earthworm, chimpanzee, and whale – springs from the same source, each of *them* is also kin.

And when we find that the separate particles that constitute dandelions, chimpanzees, whales, and humans had their beginning in the incredibly hot plasma that first issued forth from the singularity, we see how deeply and spiritually connected we are not just to our fellow earthlings, but to everything in existence.

Science has no specific answer to the question of what happened in those primordial seas to kick-start the process of life. This mystery may never be completely solved. And perhaps we are ultimately richer by having both scientific fact and the Great Mystery in our lives.

ALL OUR RELATIONS

The odds against all this life ever happening are staggering. One in how-many-million chances? Yet here we are, at least one planet in the vast universe literally humming with life.

Life has evolved over millions of years into an incredibly large and diverse entity. Countless species that called the Earth home disappeared during the five major prehistoric periods of extinction and were replaced by countless others. Today, scientists are unable to get a real fix on how many species are in existence.

In his book *The Diversity of Life*, Edward O. Wilson states there are 69,000 *known* species of fungi, with an estimated 1.6 million in existence. When it comes to all life forms, including bacteria, Wilson and other scientists are unable to make an accurate estimate of the number; Wilson hazards that it could range from 10 million to 100 million species.

We belong to such an incredibly vast, diverse, and complex family that it boggles the imagination. If planet Earth is the only place in the universe where life exists, it certainly makes up for its uniqueness by putting forth an almost infinite variety of life. All of us diversified life forms share this one planet in an intricate network of symbiotic relationships that support individuals, species, and ecosystems. Those relationships change over the eons as different species come and go. The fact that the planetary community is always in flux makes our kinships even more precious.

Many human cultures acknowledge and celebrate their kinship and interdependency with the rest of life. Although that awareness and celebration is not prevalent in our own contemporary society, there are still many who keep that concept of kinship alive.

I met such a person in Cerro de Pasco, a troubled Peruvian mining town situated at 14,000 feet in the Andes Mountains. Juan was raised in that rocky, barren land where little grows. He lived a hard and difficult life, working long hours for very little money in nearby silver and copper mines, abused and exploited as his people have been for centuries. He had every opportunity to become bitter about life, yet he raised his beer in salute to us *gringos* when we entered the local tavern, shouting out, "We are all brothers and sisters under the eye of God!"

When he realized we had no drinks with which to share in his salute, he bought us a round and made his kinship pronouncement again. This time, with a light dancing in his eyes, he included all the beasts and plants. His proclamation caught my attention and since then I have seen many examples of the truth of his statement. That truth – that all life is interconnected and part of the same Creation – was more widely accepted by early peoples like the Celts and Druids. And indigenous peoples in many lands have always viewed other beings as part of their family.

There is a North American indigenous people's prayer that sums up our connection to the rest of life. It simply says, "All My Relations!" *(Mitakuye Oyasin.)* This Lakota prayer acknowledges the sacredness of all life. It is uttered during a wide range of ceremonies and rituals and has been adopted by people of many cultures. It is often spoken four times in succession, while facing each of the four directions of the world, and is both a celebration of life and a reminder that what we humans have here is not dominion but interdependency. Without all our relations, where would we be?

Dialogue #2 Stocks Meadow Series Kalnin. 89

DIALOGUE; 1989
JIM KALNIN
CHARCOAL ON PAPER; 76 X 107 CM

4

The Spirituality of Our Kin

Uneasy Relations

The young black bear picked its way methodically through the small mountain community, going from one pile of compost to another. Our three dogs bounced around it in a frenzy of barking. Whenever we heard the dogs, we gathered to watch the bear from a safe distance.

The dogs would race in toward the bear, snapping at its hindquarters and barking. At times they were more brave than smart; Shadow got smacked in the ribs by that bear at least once. I watched her lunge dangerously close on numerous occa-sions; the bear narrowly missed her as it charged back. Those images of bear and dog attacking one another were so impressed in my mind that they eventually made their way into my drawings.

Those bear encounters gener-ated tensions and serious discus-sions in our little community. Although we respected the bears' right to live in the highlands, their presence caused concern, especially for the safety of our children. Reas-surances that black bears were sel-dom known to attack humans did nothing to ease those fears. But our

prevailing belief in stewardship of the land and its inhabitants, rather than ownership, kept us from giving in to the urge to get a gun and blow the problem away.

The persistence of our dogs eventually eased the tension. Though the bear tried its best to ignore them, the dogs were relentless in their attacks and even scored the occasional hit. Eventually, the yearling bear stopped coming around, perhaps reaching the conclusion that rotting vegetables weren't worth the trouble.

As the tail end of summer rolled into a crisp, bright autumn, peace was restored within the community. The bear was absent from the area, though not from our thoughts. During breaks from collecting firewood or harvesting the gardens, our conversations often iterated our admiration for its strength, speed, and cleverness. We didn't realize then that the young bear would soon become one of the main topics of conversation.

One October night I was lulled to sleep by the drumming of heavy rain on my roof, only to come quickly and fully awake at the sound of a loud crash, followed by the splintering of glass. I sat up in my small loft bedroom and peered down through the window into the unfinished addition I was building off the back of the kitchen. I could just make out a large black shape moving slowly through a tear in the polyethylene sheeting that served as a temporary window between the kitchen and the new addition. I could hear more banging and glass breaking and I started yelling at the bear. That did the trick; the bear pulled back out of the hole in the sheeting and ambled off.

I waited awhile, and when I could hear no other sounds apart from the drumming of the rain, I headed downstairs to survey the damage. Glass jars, spices, and containers of dried food had been scraped off the kitchen counter through the hole in the polyethylene into the unfinished room. The door I was intending to install there had been knocked over and its window broken. I cleaned up a bit and went back to bed.

When I went out to the yard in the morning I found more damage. I had left a few small apples on the front passenger seat of the car and both windows open a crack. Part of one apple was still on the car seat. One car window lay in tiny shards on the ground.

I pictured a large, wet, black bear standing in the rain beside my car, snout to the gap in the window, smelling apples. The bear would have had no trouble inserting its powerful claws into the opening and yanking the window out. It would have also done this undisturbed and unperturbed, as the dogs had been huddled in dry corners around other buildings. Because of the heavy rain, they could neither hear nor smell the bear and they never woke up.

Apart from me, no one else in the community had heard the bear. Concern grew again. But so did our respect. The bear had learned from its previous experiences with the dogs and had waited for an opportunity to try something else. Whether or not it had come to a reasoned conclusion about the ability of the rainstorm to mask its smell and sounds, it had still used that rainstorm to advantage. Even if bears are not capable of putting thoughts together and coming to rational conclusions, they still learn from their experiences.

The anxiety of that time is long gone, and what remains for me now is an odd feeling of having been blessed. Blessed, because those frequent encounters with such beautiful and powerful animals were important personal learning experiences. Like others there, I was forced to face my own fears. My reactions in those situations often brought me completely into the present moment, fully aware of not just the bear but of everything else around me.

I was also blessed to have spent quality time in the presence of bears. Bears, along with other creatures, can serve as inadvertent spiritual guides, if and when we are ready for their lessons.

Animal behaviourists and other research scientists are discovering more information relating to how animals function. Some of their discoveries concur with what people in Earth-based cultures have known for millennia: that intelligence permeates all life forms yet manifests in ways that don't necessarily fit our definitions of it. However, my scruffy old Coles Dictionary states that intelligence is "the ability to learn or understand from experience," and "the ability to respond successfully to a new situation." Both definitions fit that young bear perfectly.

The ability to respond successfully to a new situation is evident in everything from bears to houseplants to viruses. I once concluded

A magical presence is created when one truly lives in harmony with all living things.

– S. Grace Mantle

75

that mosquitoes learn from their mistakes and communicate with each other.

The renovations I was making on my house in the mountain community left openings for both large and small creatures to enter. I soon developed a bedtime ritual where I patrolled the house with a fly swatter, intent on eliminating the small whining insects that kept me from my sleep. After several nights of mosquito hunting I began to notice a peculiar pattern.

The first two or three mosquitoes I killed each night were easy targets, but the remaining ones became progressively harder to hit. By the time there were only a few left I only had to *look* at a mosquito resting on a wall for it to fly away. I began to pay closer attention to this trend and soon became convinced that they had been warned that I was after them, either by each other, or by my intention, or both.

Whether mosquitoes have mental telepathy or not, the fact remains that there are numerous forms of communication and awareness in the world, many of which we do not understand.

Recently I was told of a cat that apparently had psychic powers. It had been living in a long-term care facility for elderly people. Caregivers there began to notice that when someone died, the cat had previously been lying on that person's bed. They watched the animal more closely and realized it would go to someone's bed a day or so before they expired and remain there until the person passed. The cat continued to do this for many years without fail, to the point where the staff began to rely on it to let them know when a patient was near the end.

Events of this nature don't fit a conventional, scientifically backed interpretation of reality. I find that I neither believe nor disbelieve such stories, but instead revel in the fact that there are things in the world that are difficult to explain. The many mysteries in life help to keep it interesting.

The mysterious forces that brought the universe into existence are evident in the inexplicable workings of everything from mosquitoes to galaxies. Could it be that the Divine grace and wisdom that created the universe and keep it functioning are also the guiding forces that enable mosquitoes to know they are being hunted? Perhaps this is how a young black bear got the notion of working the night shift, and a cat intuitively knew where it would sleep. The more I watch plants, animals, and the Earth itself adapt and change, the greater is my sense of awe, and the more certain I feel that Divine will is behind each form and action.

Science strains to find logical explanations for life's mysteries. We

are told that dark matter, which makes up about 90% of the known universe, is the source of the gravitational forces that hold galaxies together. Yet that explanation may do little to diminish our wonder that the universe exists at all.

The adjective "spiritual" is described in my dictionary as being "of the spirit." We generally think of "spirituality" as being a human state of awareness, yet everything in creation is essentially a part of the Creator, or "of the Spirit."

The singularity that manifested as the "Big Bang," or the flaring forth of the universe, created a physical realm where none had previously existed. "Created out of what?" we might ask. The only logical conclusion I can come to is that matter itself is a manifestation of the Divine. That would be *all* matter, the stuff of stars, bears, and mosquitoes, as well as humans. And that would make *everything* in existence "of the Spirit," or spiritual.

Even Animals Get the Blues

Animals exhibit a range of emotions. Otters will spend hours sliding down mudbanks or tunneling into snow. This may be how they learn specific survival techniques, but anyone who watches them will no doubt come away smiling at the joy that is expressed in their actions. Wolf and lion cubs, and even their domesticated cousins, the kittens and puppies we raise as family pets, grow up wrestling with each other as training to become predators. Learning these practical survival skills also seems to be fun.

I once watched a young black bear lying on its back in a swamp. It had all four feet sticking up into the air and was scratching its hind feet with the claws on its front feet, possibly to relieve an itch. It was huffing gently to itself in a rhythmic way that seemed to exhibit great pleasure. That bear was so engrossed in its scratching that it

took some time for it to realize there were humans standing by a truck on the hillside logging road, hooting with laughter at its play. It had been so immersed in its sensation that it had completely blocked out our sounds and movements. When it became aware of us, it immediately got up and ran away.

As well as pleasure, animals also experience varying degrees of fear, anger, and sadness. I would say they are as capable of experiencing "the blues" as we are. The black bear in the barrel trap at our tree planting camp in northern Alberta didn't growl at us when we went close to observe it, but it did moan in a very sorrowful way. Bears don't growl, except in movies where growl sounds are added to make them appear fierce. But they do moan whenever they are afraid. That bear in the trap sang the blues as well as any human I have heard.

An experience I had many years ago definitely falls under the sub-heading of *Even Animals Get the Blues.* While in the city of Bang-kok, I visited the zoo. I expected to meet unfamiliar creatures indig-enous to Southeast Asia, and I did see the prehistoric muntjac deer, also known as the barking deer, for the first time. I also saw elephants. I was most intrigued by a sign, written both in Thai and English, which advised visitors that the ele-phants sometimes picked up rocks with their trunks and threw them at the spectators. The elephants instantly gained my respect when I learned about their response to being watched. That day, though, they seemed content to just stand around and doze.

I then wandered across the open area to a cage that held a raccoon. Being indigenous to North and South America, it was quite famil-iar to me, although no doubt it seemed quite exotic to most of the other visitors to the Bangkok zoo.

As soon as the raccoon saw me, it chirruped and ran up to the wire mesh. It stood on its hind legs in front of me and made its stress call. It seemed to expect something, but I had no idea what. I watched it for a while, and then started to leave. The raccoon ran beside me on the other side of the mesh until it could go no farther, then reared up again and called even louder while clawing at the cage. I stopped again, quite puzzled.

I thought it might be begging for food, but there was fruit in a dish in its cage and it seemed well fed, so I wasn't sure. This animal seemed quite upset.

The more I watched, the more certain I became that it was pleading with me, and it suddenly came to me that the raccoon wanted me to let it out of its cage. I told myself that was absurd, but the idea wouldn't go away. I certainly empathized with its predicament, as I had with that of the rock-chucking elephants. The cage didn't look impregnable, but what would happen if I let it out? I couldn't take it with me, yet how would a North American backwoods animal ever survive in Bangkok?

I was unwilling to leave it, so I stood there for some time talking to it and watching it. Its eyes never left me. When closing time came and I finally had to go, it was one of the hardest things I've done.

Animals are complex beings. This is evident to many pet owners as well as to those who have bears and coyotes as neighbours. For me, the stories in this chapter continually remind me that I live in a universe that exudes mystery. Seeing the complexities that our neighbouring life forms exhibit deepens my sense of kinship with them, and that to me is an important part of my own spiritual growth.

Encounters with the creatures that share this planet are important learning experiences. The walls that exist – in our minds as well as in our zoos – between humans and the other inhabitants of the Earth may keep us from harm, but they also limit our experiences and our sense of kinship.

We have grown up thinking of much of the natural world as vermin, weeds, germs, and pond scum. The attitudes these labels imply still direct much of our relationship with nature. Our culture brims with myths that feed our uneasiness with the natural world, from the serpent in the Garden of Eden to the Big Bad Wolf.

We are living in precarious times, with more questions than answers concerning our future. The difficulties we face will not be easily solved. We need all the help we can get to find solutions for our planet-wide dilemmas. Learning to accept all of life as our kin and indeed as our equal might bring us to a perspective where changing things seems less of an overwhelming burden. Daily awareness of our place in the web of diversified life might start us on the path to a sustainable and joy-full life on Earth.

Seeing grace in humanity is not always easy, yet we all are "of the Spirit." Recognizing that same Spirit in bears, bats, and bacteria is crucial to changing the current downward spiral of our stewardship of life on Earth.

There are signs that humanity is becoming more aware of its kinship with all life. Scientific research daily reveals new ways of understanding the mysteries of life on and beyond our planet. These discoveries allow us to adopt new attitudes about ourselves and the tenuous bubble of life-support that surrounds us. The more we know about what goes on in each small corner of our planet, the more precious and less fearful it becomes.

Each time we recognize and accept our own spirituality and that of all our kin, we remove some of the walls between us and open to deeper levels of awareness. Focusing on our commonalities rather than our differences is part of the creative process. As a race, we are still learning that a benefit to the smallest creature is a benefit to all. The more we do for each other and everything else around us, the more we do for ourselves.

With a little luck and a lot of effort, we might some day find ourselves working in cooperation with the rest of nature rather than in opposition to it.

Our task must be to widen our circle of compassion to embrace all living creatures, and the whole of nature in its beauty.

- ALBERT EINSTEIN

5

Dancing on the Rooftops

The Delicately Balanced Garden

For years I have hiked the network of trails that dissect the deep, wooded valleys and alpine terrain of southern British Columbia. When I lived in Vancouver I made regular pilgrimages with friends to alpine regions in two provincial parks. On some of those treks we laboured under heavy backpacks loaded with enough supplies for a week. We usually chose hiking routes that led to small lakes or good creeks where we would set up camp and then day trip to the surrounding countryside. Being in the wilderness both lightened and filled us in ways the city never could.

The short summers in high country mean that most flowers bloom pretty much at the same time. We hiked for hours on narrow trails through fields of blossoms, with bumblebees and hummingbirds often attracted to our fluorescent orange backpacks. Rocks littered the ground. A few stunted trees were mere tokens of the forests in the valleys below. The wind blew constantly across the land under an expansive sky. We felt as if we were walking on the very roof of the world.

When you walk across the fields with your mind pure and holy, then form all the stones, and all growing things, and all the animals, the sparks of their souls come out and cling to you, and then they are purified and become a holy fire in you.

– Hasidic saying

85

Hawks make good use of those winds as they sail along cliff edges in search of food. On one hike we were stopped in our tracks as a falcon soared into view. It glided past us on outspread wings, then suddenly tilted and dove, disappearing behind the grassy rise just ahead of us. Before long, it rose up again with something dark and still in its claws. We watched in silence until it vanished into the distance.

Life is given for life. A thriving population of alpine rodents allows a smaller population of falcons to survive. Both species live in balance as individual parts in a web of interdependency. This dance of give and take is a fundamental truth of life on Earth.

Everything in an alpine meadow is adapted for survival. Eons of long, harsh winters have shaped the species that live there. The insect, bird, and rodent populations are keyed to the rhythms of the vegetation, raising their young and harvest-

The winds have their way in this open land. Nothing impedes them as they race each other across the meadows, leap high over the mountains and course down through canyons into the lowlands. They distribute pollen, seeds, and microbes, and deliver the life-giving rains and snows. They are a vital part of the respiratory system of the planet.

ing food for winter more quickly than their counterparts in warmer climates. The large predators are also very closely linked to their environment, and mating, rearing offspring, and surviving winter are tightly attuned to the cycles of other animals, plants, and weather. Small aberrations can be fatal.

Any changes imposed on the land here can be cataclysmic. A verdant meadow can be quickly eroded away to a gravel escarpment. The park rangers and naturalists insisted we hike and camp only on their trail networks. Our youthful and rebellious natures bridled at such rules, but we soon came to appreciate the reasons for these regulations when we learned how easily the meadows could be destroyed.

Basically the same mechanics build soil everywhere, but in high meadows the balance is more delicate and vulnerable to damage. Here, ground squirrels tunnel and burrow into the thin soil, deposit-

ing their long, snake-like mounds of excavated material on the surface. That stops the soil from compacting under winter snows so that plant roots and water can penetrate. The tunneling also adds oxygen to the soil, essential for the process of decomposition of living matter into plant nutrients. The subsoil the rodents bring up to the surface gets mixed with dead plant matter and animal excrement to further enrich the garden. Efficient gardeners, those squirrels.

If we collapsed the ground squirrels' tunnels they would move away. If they deserted the sloping meadows most of the plants would die and the meagre soil would soon wash away. A camping spot we might make in the middle of a beautiful flower garden would likely be a dead spot by the following summer. With luck, the erosion wouldn't spread to destroy all of the meadow.

So we curbed our youthful spirits and stayed on the trails and in designated campgrounds. The fragility of those highlands and the importance of each part to the whole hit home with us. The cold winds, sinuous mounds of bleak earth, and squirrels and falcons reminded us that the bigger garden – the whole planet – is also in fragile, precarious balance.

Our rambunctious hikes were much more than good exercise and lessons in ecology; they often brought me back to the sensation of walking on the rooftop of the world. That perception would sometimes shift and broaden to one of walking on the surface of a planet; a planet that is floating in space, orbiting a star, adrift in a galaxy that is itself a small part of an ever-expanding and ever-changing universe.

That profound realization brought with it a sense of awe I had never felt before, along with deep gratitude. Looking back at those journeys, I think this awakened awareness was why I kept going back.

Arctic Transition

The best place I know of to experience the sensation of walking on a planet moving through space is on Baffin Island, in the Canadian Arctic. As conducive as alpine meadows are to inspiring that awareness, the open tundra is more so.

The town of Cape Dorset, on the south end of this vast arctic island, lies well above the treeline. The few squat buildings hug the lowlands, and no vegetation interrupts the rocky horizon. In winter the treeless landscape shows very few signs of life. Before going to Baffin Island to live and work, I heard the place described as "halfway between Tibet and the moon." When I arrived and saw for myself, I felt that description to be quite accurate.

For me, the bleak landscape was captivating, winter and summer alike, and when I was out in it I often had the sense that the rest of the universe was hovering just above the atmosphere, barely out of sight. If the snowy owl gliding silently over the grey rocks were to have veered off and disappeared into space, I wouldn't have been surprised.

But that owl didn't become an extraterrestrial; it just dove into a hollow and flew back up with a large rodent hanging from its claws.

"Cousin of the falcon," I thought, remembering the predator from the alpine meadow. That owl and its prey were one of many signs that the constant struggle for survival and the tenuous balance of life also exist in the Arctic.

Yet as hostile and difficult as that land can be, it also holds a surreal beauty that transcends the hardships. The islands and peninsulas of the Canadian Arctic consist largely of granite rock that was thrust up into mountain ranges about four billion years ago and subsequently ground down into undulating plateaus. That rock, covered thinly with ice in winter and polished with sunlight in summer, glows in the low arctic light. At times, the glow seems to come from within the land.

The glaciated rocks are now mostly covered in lichen, the purveyor of life in rocky, barren lands. This pioneer prepares the way by eroding the rock and creating soil. A motley collection of short, tough plants follows it, growing where they can, occupying depressions, lowlands, bogs, glades, and any small cracks in the rock where dirt has collected.

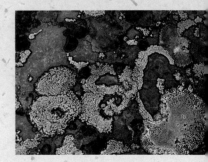

Lichens are also the main food source for the migrating herds of caribou, which in turn support many other life forms, including humans. Some lichens, like rock tripe and reindeer moss, were also important food items for the Inuit, before Western civilization caught up to them and introduced them to chocolate bars and pizza.

Plants and animals indigenous to warmer climates live in the Arctic as well, although in surprisingly altered forms. The willows growing in Beacon Hill Park on Vancouver Island are grand creatures. Their numerous drooping branches shade large areas of lawn or small ponds. The willows growing along a silted creek in the highlands of Guatemala are much smaller than the behemoths in Victoria. They grow in low, ragged hedgerows in the narrow valleys rather than as tall, stately individuals in manicured parks.

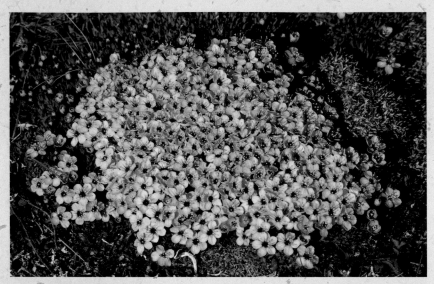

Plants in the Arctic must adapt more than their shapes in order to survive. Most arctic plants are perennials; the growing season is far too short to accommodate the complete life cycle of a flowering annual. They also tend to grow in densely packed clumps in order to retain the heat that is needed for photosynthesis to occur. These dome-like plant clusters become efficient little survival greenhouses. Thick skins and abundant hairs on all parts of the plants also work to trap solar radiation.

Everything in the Arctic grows as close to the ground as possible, to be out of the killing winds. Thus willows, and anything else that might be a tree in warmer climates, become ground cover, or at best a low shrub. The trunk of a dead willow I saw propped up against the side of a house in Cape Dorset was about two inches in diameter and three inches tall. The branches spread out from it into a flat circle, six feet in diameter. Small branches curled off the larger ones in a filigree pattern that embodied both strength and beauty – the perfect arctic mandala.

Their determination to survive in such harsh situations is inspirational. That determination reminds me, oddly, of water boatmen pelting a pond in order to further their kind, or dragonflies and butterflies enduring traumatic change for the same reason. The will to survive can take diverse forms, each one a vivid expression of the Spirit present in life.

Since my stay in Dorset started in the dead of winter, it was a while before I got a chance to study the plant life. Meanwhile, the spectacular winter and the hardy people who long ago learned to survive there commanded my attention. As I got to know some inhabitants of the mostly Inuit population of Cape Dorset, I also learned a new appreciation of ice, snow, and sub-zero temperatures. While out walking one afternoon with my Inuit friends from the Sikusilarmiut Film Workshop where I worked, a severe and peculiar snowstorm blew in. We stood on a ridge and watched the town completely disappear. We seemed to be standing in a void of howling whiteness. Knowing home was still there, within relatively easy reach, was little comfort. We endured the whiteout as long as we could, then slowly and tentatively felt our way down the rocky slope into the town. We went inside to wait out the blizzard.

When it had abated, we opened the door. We could see nothing outside; the doorway was completely sealed by a thin, hard film of snow. When we poked at the crust, a plate-sized piece fell out. We broke the hole bigger and took turns looking out at a scene of dreamlike beauty. Everything in the community was coated in the same white shell. We made a bigger hole and stepped out into what seemed like a different world – perhaps one situated halfway between Tibet and the moon.

The Inuit lived cunning and legendary lives on the land for generations. Some of the elders I met had been born into their traditional ways, before government administration and Western culture were thrust upon them and the old ways died out. Most of the young Inuit I worked with were lost somewhere between an old culture that no longer exists for them, and an attractive, alien new culture they were trying desperately to embrace. The advantages of modern Canadian culture represent only one side of a double-edged sword.

"Those were the hard days, but those were the good days," was a refrain often heard among their parents' generation, some of whom would likely give up oil heat, insulated buildings, and packaged food to return to a time when their lives were their own.

While I easily made friends with these people, I also found it hard to watch their culture die. And the sadness I felt was also for my own culture. Seeing the Inuit's alienation from their environment and their heritage brought into focus my own sense of loss. We who are part of "Western civilization" are even more disconnected from our roots than the present-day Inuit. Many of us seem to have lost *all* awareness of our connection to the land and our continuing dependence upon it.

Arctic Lights

When June arrived and the spectacular blizzards of winter took a three-month hiatus, I was able to spend much more time out on the land. At first, I travelled with my friends and their families on hunting, fishing, and berry-picking trips. Eventually though, I learned reasonably safe ways of taking day trips alone.

One early hunting trip was by motorboat to a traditional nesting ground for Canada geese. We arrived just as many of them were returning from their annual southern odyssey. After the boat deposited us on the rocks, we spread out and walked inland toward the cacophony of sounds. I had previously learned to stay close to the local inhabitants in order not to get lost, so I followed the father of one of the filmmakers up over some rocks and down again toward the marshland breeding grounds.

Neither of us spoke, as we knew very little of each other's language. Eye contact, nods, and gestures said all that was needed. We walked at ease, the hunter carrying his rifle and I my camera as we picked out a path toward the nesting area. My guide seemed to grow in stature with each step he took. Walking slightly behind him I could see a transformation taking place in him. He was out of the white man's town and in the place of his ancestors, a part of the land. And, I realized, we were out where I needed him more than he needed me.

We crested a hill and stood overlooking the marshlands, watching as more geese arrived. The air filled up with the shapes and sounds of the giant birds, until their anxious honking calls drowned out every other sound. Their excitement was a palpable thing and it affected both of us, though the hunter more dramatically.

He shot no birds that day. I felt caught up in his simple reverence and took no pictures. We sat on the rocks and watched the geese until all gunshot ceased, then we walked in silence back down to the group gathering by the boat.

Later that summer the Pootoogook family took me on a short boat ride along the coast to a small cove. We left the outboard on the beach and hiked up to the remains of an ancient settlement that had been built by the Tunit (or Dorset Eskimos, as archeologists call them).

The Inuit, who inhabit these lands now, have only been here about 1100 years. Originally from Alaska, they quickly spread east across the Arctic as far as Greenland. As they moved eastward, they found the land already inhabited by a race of larger, stronger, yet quite docile people, whom they named Tunit. The Tunit race was already in decline when the more technologically advanced Inuit arrived, and the last members fell to small-

Many birds were now within his range, and we could hear gunshots all around us, yet the Inuit man beside me stood quietly and kept his gun held loosely by his side. Then he slowly raised his free arm above his head and greeted the birds, welcoming them home.

pox brought by European whalers in 1902.

While the Tunit are gone, small pieces of their story remain. The site we visited was estimated to be 500 years old. In it were the remains of low rectangular walls of stacked stones. Originally the stones would have been roofed with whale rib bones or driftwood and covered with animal skins, likely walrus. There were some long bones lying on the ground, possibly from a bowhead whale, the largest one prominent in that area. The land around the campsite was lush with grasses and flowers, an indication that nutrients had been added to the soil through countless years of human occupation.

There was also another rectangular structure made from stacked stones that had been built against a rock promontory. The promontory had one vertical side that was relatively flat. Smaller rectangular rocks were stacked into walls off that rock face, creating an oblong stone "box." A large and heavy flat slab of stone was laid over the open top as a cover. Kananganak told us this structure would have been used as a food larder.

It took the strength of us all to slide the lid back a bit so we could look inside. We peered in to see a full-sized human skeleton lying there.

The constant chatter of our group suddenly dried up. No one said a word. We stared at the ancient remains, which in turn stared back at us. The older family members may have known what we would find, but hadn't said so. I thought of times of starvation in this camp, and of hard decisions being made for the survival of those that remained.

We stood in silence for a while, caught in our own thoughts, before closing the lid of the food cache. We roamed the old camp a little longer, then trekked inland over the low hill to a small lake that sparkled brightly under the arctic sun.

Cape Dorset is situated on a small island, about four or five kilometers in diameter, that is attached to Baffin Island at low tide. This meant I could hike there without getting lost. Or rather, if I got lost and kept my wits about me, I could follow the coast and eventually find the town again. The polar bears that roamed there in winter had moved north by then, so the risks in hiking alone were fairly minimal. I quickly got hooked on my solo jaunts across the top of the island, where the rest of the universe felt so close at hand.

Hiking alone made it easier to study the plant life burgeoning around me. Each new clump of purple saxifrage or mountain avens stopped me in my tracks. I hovered around the flowers with my camera, much like the bumblebees that depended on them for survival.

Ravens shadowed me and occasionally snowy owls were my guides.

Finding lemming nests lined with bits of black plastic garbage bags and pink fibreglass insulation was a shock at first, but they reminded me that life continues to adapt and evolve. No doubt those nests were quite warm with the triple insulating layers of plastic, fibreglass insulation, and snow.

Roaming for days on the tundra took me to many places I had never been before, both on the island and in myself. My bond with the Earth deepened with each hike. I felt a part of that cold land, and that feeling grew to encompass the rest of the planet and all that dwells there. An inner peace grew in me as I walked the open, windblown places.

On one walk I found the small lake above the old Tunit camp. Delighted, I made my way down to the site again. I couldn't move the stone slab on the food cache by myself; nor did I feel the need to. But I did feel compelled to stay awhile in that place that had opened a door into the past for me.

As I sat on a rock and watched gulls wheel about their nests on the nearby cliff, I felt kinship with those ancient humans. I thought about their lives, and could envision them walking in and out of the camp. I imagined them scaling the cliffs to steal gull eggs, as the present-day Inuit still do occasionally, or shouting and laughing as they brought pieces of whale up from the beach – that whale whose bones lay beside me, and whose flesh and blubber meant the camp would eat well for a while.

I visited the Tunit site a few more times after that, and each time the feeling of kinship grew. Sitting in the low arctic light above the food cache that was also a tomb, I felt as if I belonged there. I started to think of myself as part of the human tribe. The tribe that for so long was, and in reality still is, an integral part of the Earth. This sense of being a part of the continuous human family comes and goes. When it is with

me, mainly when I am in the wilderness, I never feel alone.

The more time I spent there the more I felt at peace. Buoyed by a sense of connection to the Inuit, and the Tunit before them, I was becoming more aware of being an integral part of the universe. The open view and the solitude I enjoyed helped nurture that awareness, as did my bond with the ancient inhabitants of that place. Those nomadic hunters of long ago travelled under the same stars. They paused to stare up at the same wheeling galaxies, likely with the same awe and reverence that I felt. It felt good to follow their lead, and to play out on the same stage my small part of the continuing human journey.

6

The Last Piece of Paradise

O w! Augh! Not again!" yelled Paddy from the front of the dugout canoe as it slid through the dense bush overhanging the riverbank. He was crouched low with his thin arms up over his head, holding on to his hat and fending off the branches whipping by.

The 32-foot-long dugout, carved from a giant teak tree, rocked dangerously in the brown muddy water. The other seven people in the boat hung on in silence as they ducked to avoid the branches. Some of them had already tried steering and knew what I was going through.

"Well, I can't steer if you don't paddle!" I yelled back from the

stern of our boat in a lame attempt to deflect blame for my clumsy attempt at maneuvering around the river bend. "I need forward momentum to make the rudder paddle work!"

This was my first try at steering the dugout, and the skills I had acquired from years of canoeing rivers and lakes in Canada were of little help. In addition, I had bragged about my expertise and the others now expected me to be able to teach them how to maneuver this boat.

We emerged from the overhanging foliage more or less intact and drifted on. The next few bends in the river were gentler and we did

Every rainforest is different, yet all have the power to overwhelm your sense with life's sheer intensity and raw beauty.

- THOMAS MARENT

better. The mood in the boat lifted when a flock of small, bright green parrots flew overhead, screeching loudly. They elicited hooting and screeching from us as well.

We were two weeks into our six-week trip along tributary rivers in the Amazon rainforest, but it was our first day travelling in our own boat without guides. We gawked at the endless array of parrots, toucans, monkeys, turtles, and butterflies that lived there. We laughed through sudden torrential downpours and languished in brilliant sunshine.

Our group had come together in Quito, Ecuador, in 1976: Paddy, Annabel, and Gabriel from England; Jesper from Denmark; Bob, Paul, Mary-Jo, and Stephanie from the United States; and me from Canada. We had been independently exploring South America and had met by chance. Gabriel had done his homework and had managed to get a letter from the former head of the Ecuadorian

Army, Amazon division, granting us safe passage through army-held territory along our route. He also got good advice on the best place to start the trip from and which rivers to take in order to pass through the few remaining pristine forests.

We did most of our organizing in Quito, where we bought supplies, including food, raingear, and mosquito netting. We then loaded everything onto a crowded night bus and travelled over the Andes Mountains to the town of Shell Mera, where the second floor verandah of a run-down hotel became the headquarters for our last stage of preparation. That consisted largely of buying tinned and boxed food and chartering a small plane to take us east to an isolated and almost uninhabited army outpost on the Villano River.

There we hired three hunters from a local tribe to take us in their canoes down the fast flowing tributary to the town of Curaray, which was situated on the larger and slower

Curaray River. We stayed there for ten days and learned about the rainforest, the river, and each other. It was in Curaray that we bought our large dugout boat.

Most of the people in Curaray were Quechua, descendants of the former Inca who had emigrated from the Andes Mountains into the rainforest several hundred years ago. While we were in town, we also met a small party of Huaorani. The Huaorani are traditional nomadic hunters and gatherers who now live semi-permanently in primitive huts. The more settled and acculturated Quechua call them *aucas,* which means "savages." Those in Curaray considered the forest dwellers to be dangerous, a reputation derived from their fierce attempts to protect their habitat and preserve their heritage. Many of the women and children in town ran and hid when the Huaorani appeared. The Huaorani wore Western clothing at the urging of missionaries, but that didn't

do much to hide the aura of wildness that seemed to cling to them.

Henry David Thoreau once wrote that the preservation of the world is in wildness. Those words came to mind when I met the Huaorani, who embodied wildness in their every action.

We met when a group of about ten men and boys came into Curaray to trade animal pelts and live parrots. Using sign language and about three words in Spanish, Jesper traded a pair of blue jeans for a blowgun and quiver of darts. I asked the chief if I could take some photographs of them. He turned to me and looked right into my soul. Then his face beamed an expansive smile and he nodded. I happily took pictures of everyone in their group. Many months later when I was developing my films back at home in Canada, that roll had somehow disappeared. I never did find it.

It rained the day before we left, so the river was high, fast, and muddy. School had been dismissed so the children could attend the launch, and many others joined them. We loaded our large pile of gear into the boat and then, after a few handshakes and hugs, we were off. The townspeople stood on the high bank and waved as we drifted away backwards, our paddlers completely out of sync with each other. As our boat shot around a shallow bend, our last glimpse was of them all still standing together and waving goodbye. No doubt they could still hear us yelling at each other as we floated away, spinning in slow circles on the eddying river.

The dugout proved to be quite spacious and very stable, if not highly maneuverable. That was lucky, considering our general lack of expertise. Bamboo floorboards created a passable deck where backpacks, tents, and plastic buckets full of food and cameras could be piled. Tarpaulins covered the gear when rain threatened. As long as we kept the storage areas compact there was ample room left between the wide wooden seats for us. I found myself being constantly amazed that this large, stable craft had been carved from a single tree.

"Easy does it! Easy does it!" coached Paddy, one hand raised to ward off branches, the other clutching a half-eaten banana.

I fought hard with the large rudder paddle to keep us from crashing into the overhanging brush again. I had learned to start the boat turning long before we were actually in a bend, so this time only a few outermost branches slapped at us as we cruised by. One caught me across the bridge of my nose – a reminder that I still didn't have the maneuver down pat. Complementing that gentle slap was Stephanie's lilting voice singing, "I can't steer if you don't paddle."

Someone chuckled on the seat in front of her.

My earlier cranky rejoinder had become an anthem of sorts. It was usually sung as we smashed through foliage on our way around corners, no matter who was steering. Our increasing ease was allowing some humour to blossom.

Joking with each other helped us bond, but the animals we saw did

that even better. I was still feeling a bit testy about Paddy's mild criticism when a band of small monkeys swung into a nearby tree, bending it down almost to the water. Paddy started hooting at them, and the rest of us soon joined in. Visits like that one often seemed impeccably timed to break some tension that had been building up in the boat.

Early one afternoon about a week or so into our journey, our casual and continuous banter was interrupted by an odd sound in the distance. The sound soon became an enveloping roar that drowned out all other noises and seemed to follow us as we drifted along. We were curious and mystified about the source of the racket, so we docked the boat and half of us, me included, ran off into the jungle to solve the mystery. We left the sunlit river and entered a world that could have been half a planet away. Close to the river the forest grew thickly, but further in, under the solid shade of the canopy, spaces opened up

between the trunks of massive trees. It was noticeably cooler, quite dark, and somewhat eerie. The silhouetted trunks of the trees, draped with vines and bromeliads, twisted their way skyward. They then merged into the intricate lacework of the canopy. Dark shapes moved from one branch to another. The reverberating, booming roar continued to drown out all other sounds.

The only relief to the dark shapes and the gloom under the forest canopy were the brightest of flowers. Gaudy heliconias grew at intervals, with their brilliant green, yellow, and red claw-like bracts seeming too colourful and smooth to be natural. The roaring drew us deeper into the forest. Jesper, as usual, was far in the lead, with the others strung out behind him. The forest floor grew wetter. I began to lag behind, distracted by flowers or the contents of stagnant pools of water.

Jesper was the first to spot them.

"They're monkeys!" he said,

pointing up at the forest canopy. "Big black ones!"

"Yeah, but some of them are brown," added Mary-Jo behind him. Then she remembered.

"They're howler monkeys! I've read about them. It's the mature males that are black. They have this extended jaw and a bone in their throats that enlarges their vocal chambers. That's what's making that sound."

She had to shout this, of course.

That was our only close encounter with these large monkeys, although we heard them in the distance on a few occasions. The sound of their voices, which is more of a roar than a howl, touched something deep inside me – perhaps a primal connection that goes back to the time before we evolved out of forests like that one. Maybe we all have wildness stored in us somewhere, waiting to awaken to a call, no matter how civilized, sophisticated, or cultured we become.

Years later, when I learned of the devastation of parts of this deep and diversified forest by oil exploration and production, the call of the howler monkey became a lament. The destroyed jungle and polluted rivers turned their territorial vocalizations into a rainforest version of the blues.

Canoeing the Menagerie

Whenever there was nothing large, noisy or colourful commanding our attention, I would gaze at the background details of that verdant world. I would watch the spectacular range of leaf shapes and patterns as we floated by different kinds of trees, or contemplate the reflections of the clouds on the water. The swirling brown river itself could mesmerize me.

That turned out to be fortunate, as I happened to be staring into it when the biggest snake I have ever seen erupted out of the water beside our boat. Thick, twisting coils of snake as big around as my thigh emerged in a shower of water and were instantly gone again.

"Did you see that?" I yelled.

Heads snapped up out of personal reveries. "What?"

"A snake!" yelled Bob.

"Where? What snake?" yelled the others.

"I don't see anything!"

"Well, it's gone now," I said, calming down somewhat. "But it was huge, like this big around!"

I held up my hands to show its girth. Bob nodded in agreement.

No one else had seen the anaconda, but they reluctantly accepted our story. There was doubt, however, that the snake had been *quite* as big as we said. Maybe no one wanted to believe we shared the river with a snake that large. Stretched out straight, it might have eclipsed the length of our dugout canoe.

We had been told back in Curaray that it was safe to swim in deep, fast-running water. We had been assured that piranhas wouldn't bother us there as they stayed in the slack water lagoons, and that stingrays only inhabited *shallow*, fast water over a gravel bottom. Deep and moving water was okay, and as for the world's biggest snakes, they were "*no problema!*" I did notice, however, that none of us swam in the river after the anaconda appeared.

We stopped each night and camped. Sometimes, when we were sure torrential rains wouldn't raise the water level, we stayed on exposed sandbars along the river. At other times we stayed at "way stations" that the local inhabitants had established. We had been told to keep an eye out for banana plants, whose distinctive foliage and large size would indicate that a way station was at hand.

These camps generally consisted of a mooring post hammered into the river bottom, a trail up the muddy bank to a clearing, a lean-to made of sticks and banana leaves, and a rudimentary garden. The gardens grew manioc or yucca, chili peppers, limes, and bananas.

Camping nightly along the river brought us into close contact with the creatures that lived there.

The wild peccary that ran squealing through camp as we were preparing for bed surprised us and made us laugh. Then it occurred to us that something must have been chasing it. The laughter stopped and a long discussion about our relative safety ensued. In the end we didn't see or hear any other creatures, but concern

continued to hang in the humid air. Most of us had a pretty short sleep that night, and at the next camp we pitched our large communal tent made of bug netting and slept in it together. Somehow that made us feel safer, and most of us slept well.

One morning, as we were breaking camp and reloading the boat, I stood talking to Annabel beside a lean-to shelter, my hand on the ridgepole. As we chatted, I happened to notice that the broken branch end on the ridgepole was swaying slightly. When I focused on it, I saw that it was not a branch but rather the head of a small snake that had wrapped itself around the pole. The swaying head was only a few inches from my hand. I stopped talking. Annabel's gaze followed mine. I very slowly pulled my hand away, and we both stepped back.

The rest of the group became aware of the snake.

"Do you think it's poisonous?" asked Annabel, both hands clutched behind her.

"Yeah, for sure," said Jesper.

"Looks like a water moccasin," added Paul.

The small snake weaved its head back and forth in a rhythmic, flowing manner, and Paul's head moved slightly as his gaze followed it.

"Can't be," said Mary-Jo. "They don't live in South America, and I think they're a different colour to this one."

"Well, it's probably dangerous anyway. We should kill it before it bites somebody!" Paul's head stopped weaving when he said this.

"How do you know it's dangerous? Not all snakes are, you know," I countered.

"I'm going to get my camera!" Mary-Jo yelled as she ran down to the partially loaded boat at the water's edge.

Paddy moved to pick up the machete. Just as Mary-Jo returned, Paddy raised the blade and in one downward motion cut the snake and the ridgepole in two.

Fierce yelling broke out from everyone in camp.

"Nice going, Great White Hunter! You could have let me get a picture first."

Mary-Jo stared at the snake, which lay in two pieces at her feet. She kicked disconsolately at the front half. Gabriel, who liked things tidy, grabbed a stick and flipped both halves of the snake into the river. We all stood there and watched the pieces drift away.

No band of cute or funny animals appeared to brighten our mood that day.

RIVER JOURNEY
JIM KALNIN

As the trip went on, I became increasingly disturbed by some of the ways we responded to the creatures whose habitat we had entered. It became clear to me that we travel with a lot more baggage than just guidebooks, cameras, and underwear. Each of us grows up with different values, fears, and attitudes concerning nature. The episode with the snake brought our group's differences to the surface. After a few more confrontations, we came to a general agreement not to harm anything in the forest unless we were in mortal danger. That agreement held, though learning the difference between our own accumulated fears and what was real and present danger was no easy task.

One thing that touched us all was the presence of the butterflies. Whenever we rested from paddling and placed the wet oar across the gunwales, one or more large, colourful butterflies would almost immediately land on it. Florescent blue wings the size of dinner plates or much smaller florescent yellow and black ones undulated slowly as the insects drank water from the paddles.

Whenever I thought I had seen *the* most outrageous butterfly, an even wilder one would come along. Each new wing-flapping visitor to our wooden boat delighted nine inner children as we paddled along.

I could feel my spirit growing with each bend in the river and each animal encounter, though differently than it had on Baffin Island. The spirituality I had felt in the Arctic was lean and bright, like the constant wind and the glow on the land. What I felt in this verdant river-world was lush and thick; wildness that bordered on the erotic. The warm air, richly scented flowers and herbs, and constant motion of the boat all worked to ground me in the present moment. I felt fully connected to the Earth. I belonged in that diverse land of the Amazon as much as I did anywhere.

Dark Clouds on the Horizon

Dark clouds usually indicated torrential rains and high, fast floodwaters on the river, but although each rainstorm made us wary, the floodwaters never became a problem for us. However, looking back, those black clouds could have been portents of a different kind of storm.

At one point during our trip we rounded a bend in the river and came upon an oil exploration camp. Grey tents squatted in the clearing above the mudbank. Two men sat on a small floating drilling rig and watched us as we passed. When someone in our group waved, one of the men waved back, but no one spoke. Our collective mood was pretty sober for the rest of the day as we speculated on some of the changes that would likely come to this place.

We crossed into Peru from Ecuador. The Curaray River flowed on to merge with the Napo and double in width. From there on, we saw many more soldiers and much less wildlife.

The Napo River led us to the main branch of the Amazon, where we changed direction and headed upstream. Farms and homesteads became quite common as we paddled hard towards the city of Iquitos and back into the twentieth century. Ocean-going freighters plied these waters. Log booms and garbage floated by.

Iquitos is a midsized Peruvian city that was established largely by the rubber trade. No roads lead out over the Andes to other Peruvian cities, but it is connected to the rest of the world by navigable water. That and the contrast of colonial architecture and run-down shanties make it appear both provincial and metropolitan.

After almost six weeks alone in the forest with the creatures of the river, we all suffered some culture shock on our arrival, and we often expressed to each other our wish to be back on the Curaray. But hotel beds, hot showers, Chinese restaurants, and pastry shops soon won us over to the comforts of city life. We spent some time together acclimatizing to "civilization" again, then broke into smaller groups and went our separate ways. I soon lost contact with most of the people in the group, and believe the others did too. Although we had little in common, we connected deeply through the experience of our river journey. We have the rainforest in its diversified glory to thank for that.

PULLING THE PLUG ON PARADISE

The pristine Ecuadorian forest through which we had paddled is now a part of Yasuni National Park and the adjoining Huaorani ethnic reserve. It extends north to the Napo River and east to the Peruvian border. This land was set aside by the Ecuadorian government, though barely protected, and was designated a UNESCO Biosphere Reserve in 1989. It has perhaps the highest biodiversity of any region of the planet. Up to 644 species of trees have been identified growing within one hectare of land, equal to the number of tree species in all of North America.

None of us knew about that when we travelled there well before the park's formation, but experiencing the abundance and vitality of that land for ourselves touched us in ways that hearing mere facts about it never could.

It also makes the current destruction harder to take. Oil exploration sites and subsequent drilling operations are causing havoc there. Parts of the park have been destroyed because a major crude oil deposit lies beneath it.

The Ecuadorian government has a dilemma on its hands. Oil could bring the poverty-stricken nation an income of 700 million dollars a year for the next ten years. Many see oil production as the only solution to poverty, and drilling permits have already been awarded to several oil companies.

At the same time, there is also much pressure on the government, from both inside and outside of the country, to leave the oil in the ground and save the rainforest, as full-scale oil production would bring increased deforestation, water and land pollution, and species extinction.

The proposed expanded oil production would destroy the chosen way of life of the Huaorani and other indigenous groups living in voluntary isolation. Perhaps ensuring that these people and their idyllic surroundings continue to thrive is as important to the rest of us as it is to the Huaorani. If Thoreau was right about wildness preserving our world, we would all be diminished without at least one tribe of free-spirited people living in an abundant land somewhere.

In his attempt to find an equitable way forward for his country, the current president of the Republic of Ecuador has come up with a unique proposal. In a bid to gain desperately needed revenue, yet at the same time preserve the forest and its inhabitants, the government will offer bonds for sale to other nations. The purchasers will buy the oil at a cost of half of the revenue that would be expected from the area purchased. The purchasers will also agree to leave the oil in the ground. This would effectively preserve the forest habitat and creatures within it and at the same time provide financial benefit to the country of Ecuador.

Critics of this proposal call it blackmail, and I think it can reasonably be viewed as such. Equally valid is the argument that what's left of the wilderness is more precious to our spiritual and physical survival than oil and gas, and rich nations and corporations are the ones who can and should pay for it.

Self-guided journeys like the one we made have since been banned in Ecuador, but Yasuni National Park and other regions of the rainforest are accessible through organized outfitters and guides. Eco-tourism is a growing business in many parts of the world, including the Amazon. Interesting options are available from travel agencies or by surfing the web. For more information about travel options and Ecuador's oil dilemma, visit the websites listed at the back of the book. When we

go somewhere, even virtually, the experience becomes part of us, and we grow with each experience.

My six-week float through that amazing land helped me change my perspective in several ways. I feel that I grew both socially and spiritually, though my relationships with my fellow travellers took some work. Being stuck in a boat for weeks on end with people I wouldn't normally associate with was a definite challenge, until I remembered the bond I had felt with the Inuit who live on Baffin Island, and with the Tunit who were there before them, and how my sense of kinship with those cultures had expanded to include the whole human tribe, including Paddy, Jesper, Mary Jo, and the others. It took time, but I got to where I felt kinship with them, and indeed we did seem to be a small tribe drifting along, contentious at times, yet connected to each other nonetheless. I had help in that matter; my bonds with the creatures we saw and their environment made it easier to build similar bonds with the others.

I feel privileged and lucky to have known such wild places. Finding a spiritual connection to each of these vastly different environments only clarified and intensified that sense of deep connection to all. I now view floating down a tropical river, hiking an alpine meadow, and photographing my way across the tundra as forms of worship, or as geographical meditations. The open arctic space reminds me of the vastness of which we are a tiny part, while the rainforest quietly whispers intimate secrets of a rich and fecund inner life. Both speak of the grace and beauty of the Earth.

We ended our river journey wanting to be back at its beginning. The return to civilization left us longing for the joy of our earlier days of discovery. There were times in the rainforest when I thought I could be happy living there.

The appreciation I gained of the planet during that time led naturally to a growing concern for its future. Environmental awareness, like hiking or paddling through beauty, is an aspect of our spirituality. Our connection to the Creator and all creation includes the responsibility of stewardship of the garden. Working in any way to maintain and promote the strength and diversity of creation becomes another kind of worship.

7

Tire Tracks and Footprints

Both Hands on the Wheel

Monumental natural forms can bring us into a state of awe and inspire our creativity. Places like the Grand Canyon, the Li River Valley, and Niagara Falls usually create lasting impressions on those who visit them. Images from that incredible "float" through the Ecuadorian rainforest are permanently seared into my memory and surface repeatedly in my art. Yet it is not only the epic forms of nature that affect us spiritually.

The hills that border the Okanagan Valley where I now live are a very long way from the rainforests of Ecuador, in more ways than one. And although they are neither famous nor spectacular, they also inspire my art and fill my soul. I am in them often, and so my connection to them is deep. When I drive through these second growth scrub forests consisting mainly of pine, fir, and spruce trees, they don't look like much. But when I walk or stand in them, I am able to see their real beauty.

I do not have to go to sacred places in far-off lands. The ground I stand on is holy ground.

— Mary de la Valette

125

Bright sunlight breaking through close-packed trees creates vistas that appear to be made exclusively of light. I stay in one place for a while and simply absorb that glow. My sight follows the light; tiny flakes of bark and thin curved branches seem to be made of molten silver or gold. I am dazzled by the play of light and shadow on dappled grey tree trunks. Sometime I think I should be drawing or painting them, then that thought drifts away. Nothing I would put on canvas could come close to what is before me. It would lack the shifting light and my changing point of view, not to mention the smells, sounds, and atmospheric sensations, no matter how well I painted it.

I drive up to the hills in my pickup truck loaded with camping gear whenever I can. Camping there still brings me peace and a sense of belonging, even though the hills are now essentially a tree farm. And a cattle range, gravel quarry, recreational facility, and garbage dump.

All this country has been logged at least once. The forests have been replaced with monoculture plantations. The planted trees are logged as soon as it becomes economically viable. The cattle industry puts beef animals in there to graze in the summer. They winter in the open grasslands nearer the valley bottoms. Now only the open rangeland not used for cattle turns green and gold in the spring when the Okanagan sunflower, or arrowleaf balsamroot as it is also known, breaks into bloom.

Loggers, ranchers, and recreational visitors leave their footprints all over the land. All summer, campers, fishers, hunters, and off-road adventurers race up and down the network of gravel roads and through the bush. Recreational vehicles of every description pack the campgrounds, creating crowded and noisy refugee camps. Every human activity, from tree harvests to family picnics, seems to decorate the Earth with more garbage. My truck adds its share of dust and noise, and the exhaust contributes to the warming of the atmosphere. I am uncomfortably aware of these facts as I seek out the quietest walk-in lakes and emptiest campsites, where the sounds of loons and songbirds are not completely drowned out.

The sight of a raw, open wound left by clear-cut logging shocks me and diminishes the peace I seek. And these scarred, treeless lots are more than disturbances to our idyllic conceptions of nature. Removal of the forest results in soil erosion, the loss

of wildlife habitat and the "blow-down" of nearby unprotected stands of trees from high wind activity.

The snows that fall on these hills each winter, with the addition of the spring rains, constitute the water supply for the semi-arid valleys below. Snowpack that builds up under forest cover melts slowly and extends the supply of water well into the summer. The snow on the bare, logged hills melts fast and causes creeks and rivers to overflow and erode the surrounding soil. The ensuing shorter period of irrigation increases the chance of drought and forest fire. Each forest fire adds more carbon dioxide to the air. The loss of trees through fire and logging means that the forest's natural capacity to consume that extra carbon dioxide is diminished.

These forests are a blessing. They provide us with many of the resources we need to house and feed the growing population. We play and relax in them as well. The lands around us will continue to serve us if we care for them in return. Yet the single-minded desire for high profit that drives many resource-based industries leads to behaviour that results in numerous ecological imbalances. The lack of forethought in standard resource extraction practices impacts us all.

Under great pressure from many sources, some logging companies are changing the wasteful ways in which they harvest the forests. A movement towards sustainability is slowly surfacing. In many regions, businesses, governments, universities, and environmental institutions are starting to work cooperatively for the good of all, though at times the *appearance* of being environmentally sensitive seems to take precedence over the actual *fact*. It remains to be seen whether or not changes to the way we regard and use our natural resources are happening fast enough and on an effective scale.

My old truck rattles and bangs its way around bends in the gravel roads. Various kinds of wildlife run for cover at my approach. I often see the back ends of bears disappearing as they lumber into the woods. The deer usually exit the roadways far more gracefully. On one lucky occasion I surprised a half-grown cougar, one of my rare sightings of those elusive animals. Sighting a cougar or a bear on the way to an overnight camp can bring with it a small thrill of fear and a mental reminder to

put the food away. Camping with a vehicle makes doing that easy, as long as I remember to firmly close the truck windows.

Bears have come into my camp at times. I was once happily floating in a boat on a remote alpine lake and turned around in time to watch a black bear walking out of my tent. I yelled and smacked the water with a paddle, which was enough to scare it off. It ran behind a large clump of shrubbery some distance from my camp. As I came to shore, I spotted it peeking out from the bushes, nose high to catch my scent. I stayed in camp making loud noises until well after it disappeared. It took some time to get around to going to bed in the tent that night. Falling asleep took even longer.

Our fear of bears and other animals may separate us from the joys of camping. Such fear may be one reason for the brisk sales of large motor homes with solid walls and lockable doors. However, for many, camping without howls, hoots, or the mysterious snapping of twigs in the night would be a diminished experience. Those sounds are as much a part of our wilderness experience as the crackling campfire.

Although it disappoints me that I mostly see animals when they are running away from me, I do appreciate that they are at least there, and encourage their tendency to avoid humans whenever possible. Our danger to them is both immediate and long term. It is global in scale. We are reducing wildlife habitat by means other than just massive logging and burning operations. Highways, subdivisions, and oil and gas pipelines cause real habitat destruction. The recent wave of global warming is now melting the ice caps. Ironically, my fear of polar bears when I wandered alone on Baffin Island has now been completely replaced by my fear *for* them.

Such fears are substantiated by the increasing frequency of reports of animal and plant endangerments and extinctions around the globe. Some scientists and environmentalists are calling our time the sixth great age of extinction. In his book *Waiting for the Macaws,* Terry Glavin clearly lays out the hard truth of this matter.

Roughly 34,000 [plant species], or 12.5% of all the plants known to science, are threatened with extinction. One in eight bird species is threatened with extinction, along with one in four mammals, one in three of all known amphibians, four of every ten turtles and tortoises, and half of all the surveyed fish species in the world's oceans, lakes and rivers. Perhaps a million of our fellow species are trailing wearily towards that final cliff edge. We lose a distinct species, of one sort or another, every ten minutes.[1]

Our beleaguered local forests are also indirectly suffering the effects of global warming. In northern British Columbia, the Yukon, and Alaska, infestations of the mountain pine beetle are presently devastating the majority of the forests. Most of the hills I see in my travels are increasingly turning from a healthy green colour to the rusty brown of dead and dying pines.

A natural part of the landscape, mountain pine beetles were once kept in check by cold winters. The increased amount of carbon dioxide in the Earth's atmosphere has compromised this natural restraint, and

1   Terry Glavin, *Waiting for the Macaws*, (Penguin Canada, 2006)

the beetle populations have increased disproportionately. The beetles are strong fliers – swarms of them have been discovered high up in the atmospheric jet stream – and they travel rapidly to wherever pine trees are found. Adult pine beetles drill small holes through the bark and lay eggs in the layer of growing tissue between the bark and the wood. The eggs hatch into larvae that eat this cambium layer. This kills the trees.

I recently found the needles of a ponderosa pine near our home turning rust red and sagging. Close inspection revealed that the tree is infected with mountain pine beetle. I checked its neighbours, including the venerable old ponderosa next to the house. Some beetle signs were evident, which means we will likely lose those trees as well. The older pine has become a valued part of our lives. I have drawn that big tree and stared up into its branches countless times. Our son played on the rope swing tied to one of its branches. It will be sorely missed if it dies.

While I worry about one tree, the real tragedy is that we are losing many of our western forests to this epidemic. However, compared with the rapid destruction of other forests worldwide, mainly through logging and burning for land clearance, the mountain pine beetle infestations seem minor. The litany of imbalances on our planet is a long one. The thing we call *wilderness* now

exists mainly in our imagination and memory. Our footprints and tire tracks are evident everywhere, including on the moon. The increasing number of epidemics and infestations, the melting ice caps, and the rapid loss of all kinds of species are urgent indications of our need to make drastic changes.

The human race is faced with a real challenge. Any effective response to the current imbalances in the world will require a quantum shift in our collective consciousness. That would call for a change in our perception of reality and subsequently our values, attitudes, and habits.

Change of any kind is never easy. Changing the consciousness of an entire race of independent-minded beings seems impossible. We are amazingly resilient creatures who habitually resist change until there is no other alternative. Only then do we adapt. Somehow, I have faith in our ability to do that now.

Changing the way we live on and care for the Earth means chang-ing our relationship to all existence. Each small piece of the universe, including this planet, contributes to the whole through its own vital presence. We play our part in that contribution. Humanity offers its self-awareness to the whole of Creation, by which the Greater Entity can come to know itself.

Our challenge now is to enhance our awareness of our connection to everything in the whole universe; to embrace this interconnectedness as part of our self-definition and self-awareness. For that reason, as well as others, I will continue to venture into these over-burdened hills for as long as I can, to study the swamps, rivers, rocks, and deep woods. I will drive past the shorn hills and the overcrowded campgrounds so I can paddle and float out into the beauty and stillness that remain.

The path to realizing our kinship to all existence is different for each of us, yet for many it means spending more time alone, or face to face with non-human aspects of Creation.

THE ART OF ECOLOGY

As an artist I have learned that drawing the world around me can be a powerful form of prayer. It also works well for those who do not consider themselves to be artists.

The simple act of recording some small part of creation with a pencil and paper requires us to focus all our attention on it and really see that particular thing in all its glorious detail. Whenever I draw a dandelion, it becomes an amazing structure, no longer a "weed." Drawing anything – a person, a building, a forest – allows me to see beyond my attitudes, opinions, and beliefs about that thing. The object becomes another aspect of the Divine. Many people now use drawing as a means of understanding and appreciating life. Frederick Franck's book *The Zen of Seeing* is an excellent introduction to this form of meditation.

I still take along art supplies when I go camping, though I don't use them much. Mostly I simply watch the light and stare up into the tree branches. What I see burns into my retinas and my soul, and pours out later in my studio in different ways. I find that *responding* to nature rather than faithfully recording it deepens my appreciation of it. Responsive forms of art proliferate in the world now, and each one offers a different point of view of existence. However, there are also artists who can get to similar depths of understanding by faithfully recording what they see.

California artist Russell Crotty takes the classical tradition of observational drawing to new heights. He has a small observatory in Malibu where he watches the night sky and makes detailed ballpoint pen drawings of planets and galaxies. He then expands or alters these studies in his studio. Many of his finished drawings are made on paper-covered Lucite globes, some of which are four feet in diameter. Crotty has stated that the continuous acts of viewing and drawing the universe fill him with awe and gratitude.

Many artists find the glorious details of our own planet to be ample inspiration. British artist Andy Goldsworthy has become celebrated worldwide for his reconfigurations of forms in nature. He has spent hours by a stream stitching leaves together with grass stems and then photographing them as they flow down the river. The leaves become collaborative art made by trees, water, and Andy. They take part in a dance choreographed by rocks and moving water. The interconnectedness of all life is well expressed in this work.

Andy also took autumn leaves that were turning colour, wet them, and plastered them onto a large rock. Concentrating the beauty of nature in this manner brings that beauty to our attention. Those leaves have long since dried up, fallen off the rock, and returned to the soil, but the image of them lives on, photographed and printed in a number of books.

Others beside visual artists are opening avenues to deeper awareness of our environment. Musician Murray Schafer has created orchestral compositions, choral music, and various forms of musical theatre that incorporate or respond to the sounds of the world. While teaching at Simon Fraser University in Vancouver, he collaborated with colleagues on the World Soundscape Project, which initiated research into acoustic ecology. Murray's book *The Tuning of the World* elaborates on the various aspects of their research.

The world is as alive with sound as it is with anything, yet most of us automatically tune out much of what we hear. Focusing on sound is another excellent way to connect us with the present. Any step we take to increase our awareness brings us more in tune with the totality of Creation.

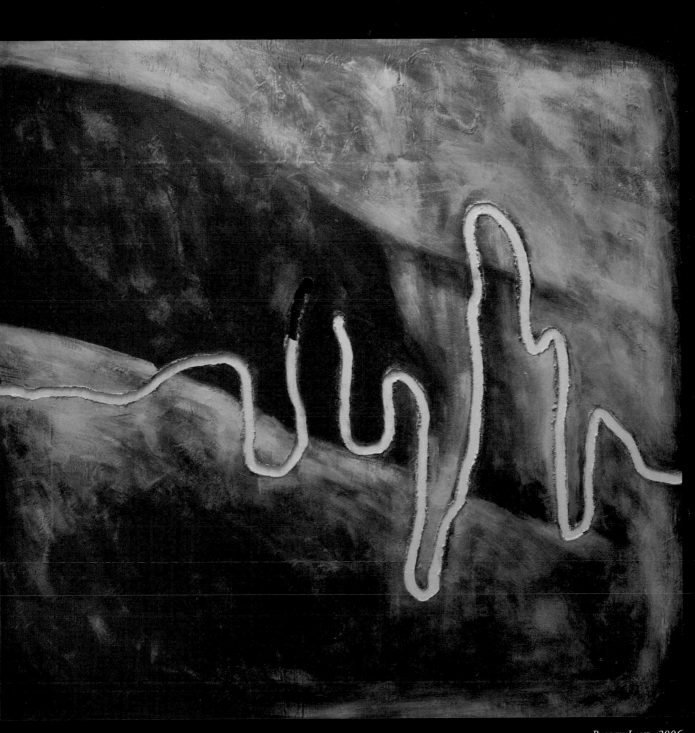

Barren Land, 2006
Aleita Manderson
2' x 4' acrylic on plywood and paper

Ecological concerns make their way into our art as well. A number of artists in British Columbia and other areas with mountain pine beetles infestations are painting landscapes with dead pine trees or making abstract paintings or sculptures that imitate the patterns the beetle larvae make under the bark of the trees. For some, this is a way of coming to terms with their changing environment.

Renay Egami, an associate professor at the University of British Columbia's Okanagan Campus, has made a number of installation art works inside chest style freezers. The freezer becomes a metaphor for the preservation of culture, memory, identity, and the environment.

In one freezer, she installed an arrangement of frozen sea animals and foodstuffs. When gallery visitors opened the freezer lid to view the interior, they activated a sound system that broadcast her father's voice singing Japanese folk songs. The food items, sea animals, and folk songs reflected aspects of Japanese culture that were a part of Renay's upbringing. When we consider the degree to which our ocean habitats are now being depleted and destroyed, Renay's installation piece is a statement not only about the loss of cultural identity but of the loss of food resources and wilderness as well. Renay finds that responses to the freezer installation project now include thoughts about

PEACEFUL PENETRATION
RENAY EGAMI

species preservation, whereas they didn't in the past.

A more recent freezer installation project incorporates ice sculptures of polar bears on ice floes. They remain intact only as long as the freezer door is closed. When we intervene by opening the door, they start to melt. The reference to the endangerment of both the bears and their habitat is quite evident in this work.

For the many artists whose personal lives inform their work to a large degree, ecological awareness is being added to the things they express. As we see species die out and we feel the effects of changing weather patterns, we become more aware that our individual lives are not isolated from the whole. What happens to polar bears and pine forests indeed happens to us all.

My friend Marilyn Raymond lives with nature all around her. The sounds and images of her fellow creatures insinuate themselves into the poems she writes about her own life. Her poems simultaneously evoke the beauty and fragility of our world, and touch on inner strife. *Frog Song* raises old alarms in a very personal way.

Frog Song

ancient and ageless
the frogs are singing
in the dark

Down the trail from my house
  the frogs are singing
their shrill swamp song echoes
  in my tiny valley
I sit on my deck in the mild dark and yearn

Tiny and vulnerable
frogs sing the worldwide songs
  of warning and celebration.
Every spring when the world is reborn
the frogs sing
  alive alive alive
  in the fading evening light.
Their shrilling voices call out
  still here
  still safe
  alive alive alive

When I was a child,
my young mother remembered
running barefoot through the dark
to the outhouse.
The warm squish
of the frog on the path
vivid in her voice.

The despairing, crushing, croak
  resounds
in my memory.

A careless moment
and the sharp sweetness of frog song
  carries an echoed edge of blood
  and death

When I was a child
my young father remembered
  playing near the swamp
  with his brother

Blowing through grass straws
  and laughing
  as frog balloons floated.

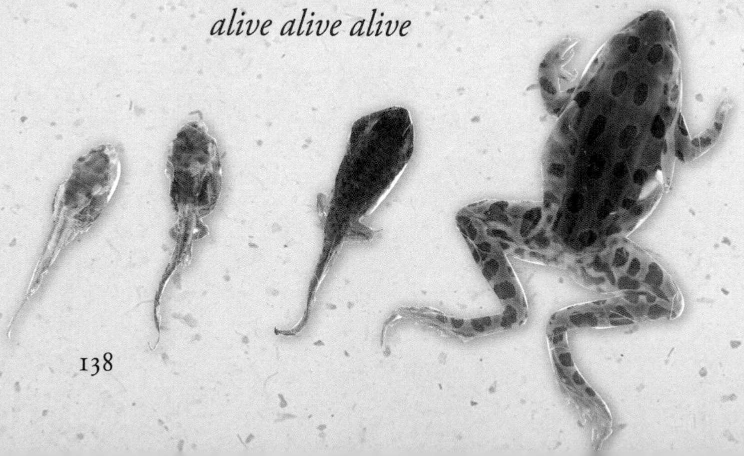

Cartoon balloons with dying frog faces
float in my memory
   stoic and helpless
    Silent

A careless moment.
A selfish, careless moment
and the heartbeat rhythm
stutters
alive a . . . live
   falters a . . . live
   stops

From my bedroom window I listen.
The frogs are singing from the swamp
The night seems large
the wild chorus
no longer fills the dark.

Dead frogs in Maritime ponds.
Frog watch.
Alert! Alert! Alert!

How could I live in a world
  with no frogs?
   No frogs singing in the dark?

The story teller,
the one who weaves the world together,
who lives under the surface of our dreams,
sings with the voices of the frogs
tells our life story
with the voices
of the frogs.

And when they stop . . .

Our various forms of creativity have long been considered bridges between heaven and earth. We might also think of creativity as a bridge to cosmic consciousness. Perhaps it is within that larger, all inclusive self-awareness that our spirituality can truly grow and blossom.

We can use different creative voices to raise alarms when they are needed. Performance art, traditional theatre, and all kinds of music now respond to social and environmental concerns, and to changing perceptions about our place in the universe. While art alone can't curtail global warming or save anything from extinction, all our creative responses can indeed function as bridges and doorways that invite us into closer contact with the world around us. Deeply knowing our kinship with all things on this Earth and in the immensity of time and space may be what ultimately saves us.

8

Returning Home

This is a path I have walked before, and one I hope to walk again. I am trudging along a dusty logging road in the waning light of day, following a beautiful river downstream to a campground. I have been on the river all day in a ritual I have performed every summer for the past dozen years. The river seems to flow in me now; this place has long felt like home.

The river sings in its bed below the shoulder of this gravel road I am following. The road curves as the river curves, though less nimbly, and then swings away up a steady grade over a low hill. After fishing upstream all day, I'm taking the easier and less interesting way back to camp.

My walk along the river this morning was long and sinuous, a convoluted dance around boulders, through shallow rapids, and by deep emerald pools,. Each bend in the river revealed new secrets; each step took me closer to the Source. I am tired now, and the no-nonsense

flat grades built for logging trucks are what I need going home.

The Kettle River flows south from the Monashee Mountains in the southern interior of British Columbia. It tumbles through the dry valley and winds its way across the border into the state of Washington. It then flows into the Columbia River on its way back to the ocean. It is another bright strand of water in the life-giving circulatory system that spans the globe.

Lois and I camp along this river every summer with about twenty friends. For a week, we live simply on the land. We cook and eat together on picnic tables under suspended nylon tarpaulins. Our lawn chairs decorate a nearby beach, or form a ring around the campfire pit. Our children came with us until they got lives of their own. Occasionally they still join us for a night or two and add their own glow to the campfire. We hike, swim, sunbathe, fish, read books, learn about nature, and play music and sing songs into the night. Reassuringly, the river flows by.

Most days we head out, in groups or alone, to explore – beaches, cliff faces, hollow logs, waterfalls, swimming holes, trails, and hillsides. My annual walk up the river with my fishing rod gets me to more places than I would go to without it, although in reality I go to visit these remote places just as much as to fish them. Reaching a hidden pool after a strenuous climb over a rock bluff is an end in itself.

A number of us hiked upriver yesterday, although not as far as I have come today. Our group included friends Susan and Barry and their two children, who are surprise visitors to the camp this year. We trudged under the hot sun, kids in tow, to the deep pool below the falls. By the time we had hiked over the bluffs and carefully picked our way down the steep trail to the long rock shelf by the pool, we were ready for a swim in the cold water.

Susan's children were cranky, resistant, and whining a steady mantra at their mother. She left them with Barry and waded along the submerged rock shelf into water up to her knees. Then she dove in.

The complex world of childhood disenchantments, sibling rivalries, and parental guilt dissolved into the cold, green underwater realm. She rose to the surface and began to swim hard against the steady current. She worked her way up to the falls at the head of the pool. Several others followed her there where, exhausted, they beached themselves on narrow rock shelves or clung to smooth boulders in the fast, foaming water. As I watched them from the cliff top, it seemed to me that a powerful magnetism of exhilaration and awe held them in place. I was reminded of the spawning salmon, pooling before the next great test to their waning stamina, as they fought to reach the place where they had begun.

I watched my friends awhile, and then moved on up the river, sometimes alongside it, sometimes in it, satisfying small curiosities. When I returned to the canyon pool, the others had gone. Faced alone, the pool seemed too big for me, an intimidating force that needed the

ported into the wordless, timeless realm that the river always offered.

I came back out here again today, this time alone, with my fly rod pointing out my path along the river. I walked beside and in the water all day, far past the deep pool where the others had honoured their kinship to salmon. I wandered to remote, shallower stretches and danced in fast water, over small rocks, and along sandy beaches. The shifting display of light was mesmerizing. Dappled sunlight filtering through green forest cover made the riffles of water pulse and glow.

I get happily lost on these walks. I lose myself in the music of water tumbling over rocks, in the splashes made by rising trout, and in the songs of small birds.

There are places where I wade out over slippery boulders into fast water or deep current, to make a better cast into a pool. I use a sturdy stick to prevent myself from being swept away. Sometimes, standing in this gleaming river, it seems almost

Where I sit is holy, holy is the ground, forests, mountain, river; listen to the sound all around me.

— Anonymous

support of numbers to be properly swum. So I moved downstream and found a smaller, personal pool in which to slake away the dust and the day's mental debris. Yet even in that shallower pool, I was trans-

incidental that I have come to fish. Fishing becomes a means of going past my own fears to get deeper into the world's primal forces. I catch a fish and release it, and think that I may eventually learn to go that deep into nature without their help.

The shifting surface of the planet has contributed to the shape of this river valley. Climate has affected the topography as well. Now humans add to its reshaping by building a network of roads and removing the forests between them. I left camp this morning along the rugged and enticing path that nature provided, and return now on humanity's smooth, convenient, and oil-soaked rearrangement of the Earth. The monotony of this logging road lulls me into a state of sleepy awareness, which is dissolved by a familiar wake-up call. A rumbling drone in the distance slowly grows loud, and the ground begins to shake. I swing over to the side of the road, knowing what's coming.

It's late now, almost dark; this has to be the last logging truck of the day, roaring by me with a full load of tree trunks recently cut from the land. The driver gears down on his approach to the hill I am still climbing. Noise and vibration engulf me. The river gets lost in the calamity.

The truck passes in a hurry, guided by a corporate rhythm that is in turn driven by the desire for high profits. When it is gone, the solitude returns. I resume my sleepy rhythmic walking through the gathering dark toward a bright campfire and family and friends.

Are We There Yet?

There are no passengers on Spaceship Earth. We are all crew.

— Marshall McLuhan

We are intelligent beings, yet we so often seem to lack wisdom and compassion. But to me, these attributes would seem to be as integral to higher intelligence as highly developed mental prowess. We are part of the planet and part of the universe, but generally we act like neither. Humanity as a whole still suffers the crippling effects of self-centredness and selective vision, evidenced by war, poverty, environmental destruction, and other forms of violence and injustice. These are hurdles we face, individually and as a species, on our physical and spiritual journey.

Accepting ourselves as belonging to the natural world seems essential to resolving our human crisis. We are now at a point of technological and scientific achievement where some people believe we can and should manage the ecosystem and direct evolution. What we haven't yet exhibited is enough wisdom or vision to be effective managers, let alone gods.

Coming to this river valley often brings certain thoughts and expectations into focus. At times

on these daylong river walks, I realize I am waiting for the human race to get its act together. I think we are capable of great achievements in all areas of life without having to sacrifice deep inner peace.

Some consider the human race to be at an early stage of development, similar to the phase of adolescence. Anyone who remembers being a teenager will recall countless incidences of impatience with the growing process. Most teens want to go out alone at night well before they are at all streetwise, and most can't wait to drive a car. Having to take driving *lessons* can seem like an incredible waste of time to someone at this stage of development. The gangly teen that we call the human race wants the car keys *right now.* "Like, what's the problem? I know how to drive!"

Youth carries with it a perception of invincibility that may be natural to that stage of development but only seems dangerous from an adult perspective. The adult who senses the danger of impatience will resist these demands and even attempt reason. But who is there among us to take the keys to the family car away from the politicians, oil magnates, and bioengineers?

There is another, similar metaphor we can use here. The impatience of youth is best embodied in the cry that emanates from the back seats of family cars everywhere: "Are we there yet?"

Impatience to reach the goal is evidenced in the many ways we ignore the view during our "journey" on this planet in our collective "family car," in our eagerness to get to where we want to be. Our goal is always somewhere along the road ahead.

Desire for personal gain which results in rampant resource depletion and the manipulation of plant and animal species by selective breeding and bioengineering are only two of numerous examples of that backseat childhood impatience.

I have a recurring vision of humanity living in a completely different relationship with the land and each other. I imagine us finally evolving to a point where everyone is fed and cared for without overtaxing the environment. In this vision, we live in balance with the whole ecosystem and at peace with all life forms, including each other and ourselves. We view all life as sacred.

The fact that there is no grand plan for achieving this utopia doesn't deter me from believing in its potential. Perhaps that is because I have faith in both our abilities and in the nature of life itself.

We live in interesting times. That ancient composite of curse and blessing has never been more meaningful than it is now. Our current difficulties may seem irresolvable, yet I do think the human race has the capability to pass through adolescence and finally come of age.

Going There

Camp is still a distance away though at times I think I can already hear Johnny's guitar and Chris's drums ringing up the valley. Supper will be over by the time I get there, but some will be saved for me. Meanwhile, the darkening road and the waning light keep me company.

Gravel roads have their own beauty when large trucks aren't commanding the space. They are a less intrusive convenience than most highways and city streets. Walking on this road often conjures up memories of distant roads in other lands. This is a tertiary road built for local and specific use, but in many places a road like this would be a major highway and likely the only land route available.

Over thirty years ago, a night bus travelling a similar gravel road carried me across the Andes Mountains from the city of Quito to the frontier town of Shell Mera. I went

there with the eight travellers I had met to begin our six-week rainforest adventure. The final leg of that journey to Shell Mera was along the Pastaza River. The river is surrounded by the green verdant carpet of the Amazon basin lapping up against the east slopes of the Andes, creating a unique environment

known as a cloud forest. I awoke on the bus at the first morning light with a stiff neck and no idea where I was. I glanced out the window and saw crystal waters tumbling over coloured boulders in a stream. This could have been the Kettle or the Skagit, or any river that I knew from my home. Then the fog of sleep dissolved and I remembered I was in Ecuador.

Two days later, in the middle of preparations for our trip into the Amazon Basin, I left the others and headed out on my own. I had a spinning rod in my hand and a daypack on my back, and I followed the Pastaza back up into the mountains.

I walked up that river with my head on a swivel, alternately gazing from the familiar to the exotic. Although the river reminded me of home, the cloud forest definitely didn't. There were banana plants and all manner of vines clinging to venerable hardwood trees with exotic names. Not one ponderosa pine in sight. Unrecognizable sounds emanated from those trees as well. I stepped off the road into the forest at one point and stared up into more shades and colours

of green than I thought could exist there. As I sat hunched, staring up into the trees and listening to the cacophony of sounds, a burst of joyous laughter erupted from deep within me. These unfamiliar places took me back to a time of youthful innocence. I saw new things through childhood eyes.

When my awe faded, the urge to fish came back. I returned to the gravel road and continued upriver until I crested a low grade and looked down onto a long stretch of the river. The water was gleaming under the tropical sun. Deep pools alternated with riffled expanses. I then realized that thick clouds were advancing and adding dramatic lighting changes to the long view of water, trees, and rocks.

I found a place to access the gravel shoreline and picked my way down. Several large mid-stream boulders were creating tumbling water upstream at the head of a substantial pool. It seemed a perfect place for fish to hang out. The pool was some distance out in the river, making it difficult to fish from the shore. I didn't know what lived in the water, but knew we were too high up in the mountains for piranha, so I waded in and over to the bottom of the pool. I was almost waist deep in moving water by the time I got to a spot where I could easily cast a spinner up into the pool.

I had fished for a while with no action and decided to move farther upstream when a large dark cloud blocked the sunlight. I watched its shadow pass over me as it rolled up the river; my attention was riveted on the steadily darkening water. The deep hues in the current were mesmerizing, even foreboding. When the sky above me was filled with clouds, they split wide open. Within minutes, another river's worth of water poured down and the top half of my body became as wet as my legs in the stream. Somehow I remembered to close my mouth and to hang on to my spinning rod. Rain fell so thick and fast I couldn't see through it. The drops hitting the surface of the river spread out into a continuous carpet of watery streaks and splashes that obscured everything and replaced it with a grey-silver realm of pulsating light.

And then the sun came out, lighting everything up. The rain continued full bore and the dark silver, shimmering field all around me turned to white and gold.

If ever in my life I expected to hear the voice of God that would have been the moment. But thoughts of any kind were beyond me. The fabric of the universe seemed in direct contact with each cell in my body, and all cognitive processes were on hold. Pulsing light and roaring sound were all that existed. Reality, beyond the dream of life.

The light dimmed as the rain lessened, and eventually I could make out the river and its shores. Then I was back in my body and mind, capable of thought, an individual person in the world again. I was a lone, wet person standing in a river, holding a fishing rod, and laughing.

I probably laughed most of the way back to town, though my memory of the return walk is dim. I tried telling the others about my experience but couldn't. Attempts would soon dissolve into laughter on my part, resulting in some strange looks.

The next six dramatic weeks that made up the journey out of Ecuador into Peru pushed my Pastaza River experience deep inside. It resides there yet. Sometimes it glows a little. Occasionally, when I stand in the colder waters of the Kettle River, an echo of that time on the Pastaza returns and my thoughts once again dissolve. Experiencing these rare occasions when I am completely immersed in the here and now, causes me to crave more of them. However, continuously maintaining that level of awareness is something I am as yet unable to do.

The universe keeps on expanding, and it takes us along with it. We came from the stars as molecular matter and evolved here on Earth into sentient life. When I walk along any of the world's gravel roads at night, the galaxies that fill the sky remind me of where it is that we all live.

This is a crucial time for life on Earth and for our spiritual growth. Many of the beliefs that humans have developed with regard to our place in the living, changing universe are now in need of revision. Our self-definitions must be expanded to include *all* of life. We need to close the gaps that exist between us as humans, and between humanity and rest of the living planet.

We need to address what is left of the wilderness from whence we came with our intelligence and our creativity. We need to nurture widespread understanding of the concept that the Earth entity exists as one being, complex in form and self-aware, and well on its way to realizing its divinity and grace. Clarity and wisdom reside in each particle of our being and we are each charged with manifesting that wisdom in all parts of our lives. Perhaps that is the true meaning of returning home.

The wave of unconditional love that pushed that pinpoint of hot dense plasma out into the void created everything in its expression. That unconditional love resides in each star in the night sky and each pebble on this road I am on. I walk this road back to camp, yet I am already home before I get there. I am a part of this place, as it is part of me; we are one being, part human, river, road, fish, truck, and galaxy-filled sky.

At night make me one with the darkness. In the morning make me one with the light.

— Wendell Barry

Humanity is made of the same molecules as the Earth that holds us. We are all parts of the Greater Being; each and everything a unique expression of the unconditional love that created life.

I hold my arms out to encircle the darkening valley as I walk, one part of Creation embracing another.

Sources

Listed here are books and websites that in some way have helped me write this book, as well as others the reader may find of interest. The people, animals, and landscapes I have encountered in many parts of the planet have also served as valuable resources, from the tallest tale to the smallest insect to the grandest canyon.

Books

A Short History of Progress – Ronald Wright, House of Anansi 2004

Amazonia – Loren McIntyre, Sierra Club Books / Douglas & McIntyre 1991

Biophilia – Edward O. Wilson, Harvard University Press 1986

Darwin, Divinity and the Dance of the Cosmos – Bruce Sanguin, Copperhouse 2007

Leaves of Grass – Walt Whitman, W.W. Norton & Company 1965

Pilgrim at Tinker Creek – Annie Dillard, Harper Perennial Classics Edition 1999

Rainforest – Thomas Marent with Ben Morgan, DK Books 2006

Silent Spring – Rachel Carson, Mariner Books 2002

Tao Te Ching – Lao Tsu Translated by Gia-Fu Feng & Jane English, Vintage Books 1972

The Great Work – Thomas Berry, Bell Tower NY 1999

The Path – Chet Raymo, Walker Publishing Company 2003

The Pond – Gerald Thompson, Jennifer Coldrey & George Bernard, MIT Press 1984

The Sacred Balance – David Suzuki with Amanda McConnell, Greystone Books 1999

The Sacred Depths of Nature – Ursula Goodenough, Oxford University Press 1998

The Tuning of the World – R. Murray Schafer, Knopf 1977

The Universe Story – Brian Swimme & Thomas Berry, HarperCollins NY 1994

The Weather Makers – Tim Flannery, HarperCollins 2006

Waiting for the Macaws – Terry Glavin, Penguin Canada 2006

Walden – Henry David Thoreau, CRW Publishing 2004

Some useful websites

www.sacredtexts.com/ane/enuma.htm

http://hubblesite.org/newscenter/archive/release/1996/22

http://apod.nasa.gov/apod/ap991122.html

www.ecuador-travel.net/biodiversity.parks.yasuni.htm

www.oilwatch.org/doc/documentos/Keep_oil_underground.pdf

http://www.vivatravelguides.com/south-america/ecuador/amazon-basin/yasuni-national-park

CREDITS

© Chris Duggan
pages 6, 124, 146

© Kai Duggan
pages 40, 44, 77, 143, 150

© Chuck Kalnin
papge 4-5, 15, 20, 30, 32, 42, 45
(bottom), 49, 142

© Jim Kalnin
pages 38, 79, 95, 101,
127 (bottom), 145, 159
page 116 *River Journey* by
Jim Kalnin.
page 70 *Dialog*, 1989 by
Jim Kalnin.

© Phil and Lee Kalnin
pages 27, 54 (bottom)

© Ralph Milton
pages 11, 26, 39, 52, 157

© Marisa Ramey
pages 14, 31, 129

© Verena Velten
pages 16, 84

© Richard Vignola
pages 78, 91 (top right), 92-93, 96

© Spiro Vouladakis
pages 9, 19, 34, 45 (top), 47, 126,
131

p. 27 © Craig Kalnin
p. 28 *Scattered Landscape*, 2003 by
Toni Onley.
© Jenkins Showler Gallery,
White Rock, B.C.
p. 41 © Lois Huey-Heck
p. 43 © Rita Baldinger. Poem by
Ruth Baldinger (age 12)
p. 68 © Barb Stephen
p. 103 © Annabelle
pp. 108-109 © Thomas Marent
p. 135 *Barren Land* by
Aleita Manderson
© Aleita Manderson

p. 137 *Peaceful Penetration* by
Renay Egami.
© Renay Egami
© photos.com
pages 100, 122, 138, 160

GettyImages
p. 1 © Riser/Paul McCormick
p. 23 © Digital Vision/Darryl Leniuk
p. 72 ©/Riser/John Kelly
p. 87 © Purestock
p. 102 © The Image Bank/
Caroline Schiff
p. 104 © Minden Pictures/
Pete Oxford
p. 113 © National Geographic/
Ed George

CORBIS
p. 51 © Clouds Hill Imaging Ltd./
David Spears
p. 61 © STScI/NASA/NASA, ESA, J.
Hester and A. Loll (Arizona State
University)
p. 63 *Ancient of Days* by William Blake
© Leonard de Selva
p. 64 © Michael Agliolo

iStockphoto
p. 2-3 © Lorenzo Colloreta
p. 10 © Miachael Lok
p. 12 © Alex Potemkin
p. 13 © Andrew Penner
p. 17 © iStock
p. 18 © Oleg Prikhodko
p. 24 © iStock (millipede)
© Pavel Lebedinsky (beetle)
© photos.com (grasshopper)
p. 25 © Sven Klaschik
p. 29 © iStock
p. 33 © Peter Zaharov
p. 36 © Jennifer Bird
p. 46 © Andrey Pavlov
p. 48 © iStock
p. 50 © Ben Blankenburg
p. 53 © Richard Mirro
p. 54 © Jon Rasmussen (top)
p. 55 © iStock
p. 56 © Douglas Allen (top)
© Glenn Frank (bottom)
p. 57 © Michael Steden

p. 58 © Jason Lugo
p. 59 © Harry Thomas
p. 60 © iStock
p. 62 © Manfred Konrad
p. 65 © Jens Carsten
p. 66 © Julien Grondin
p. 75 © Michel de Nijs
p. 76 © iStock
p. 80 © Pavel Mozzhukhin
p. 83 © Pete Smith
p. 86 © Daniel Cardiff
p. 88 © Paul LeFevre
p. 89 © Jana Fernades
p. 90 © Ryerson Clark
p. 91 © Sebastien Lefbvre (left),
© Neta Degany (right bottom)
p. 94 from top to bottom,
© Dmitry Deshevykh,
© Grant Dougall, © iStock
p. 98 © David Hutchison
p. 110 © Alex Bramwell (top),
© Nicola Gavin
p. 111 © Jacom Stephens (top),
© Amy Yang
p. 112 © Michael Zysman
p. 114 © Rob Broek
p. 115 © Robyn Glover
p. 116 © Steve Geer (butterfly)
p. 117 © Ismael Montero (butterflies)
© Eric Isselée (toucan)
p. 119 © Brandon Jennings
p. 120 © iStock
p. 121 © Ray Roper
p. 123 © iStock
p. 127 © Jim Parkin (top)
p. 128 © Alison Trotta-Marshall
p. 130 © Alex Bramwell
p. 133 © Chen-Chun Wu
p. 136 © Richard Goerg
p. 139 © Lev Ezhov
p. 140 © Dave Logan
p. 141 © Leah-Anne Thompson
p. 147 © Don Wilkie
p. 148 © Harry Kolenbrander
p. 151 © Klaas Lingbeek van Kranen
p. 152 © Morley Read
p. 155 © Evgeny Kuzmenko